THEY
ASK,
YOU
ANSWER

MARCUS SHERIDAN

THEY
ASK,
YOU
ANSWER

A REVOLUTIONARY APPROACH TO
INBOUND SALES,
CONTENT MARKETING,
AND TODAY'S DIGITAL CONSUMER

FOREWORD BY KRISTA KOTRLA

WILEY

This book is printed on acid-free paper. •

Published by John Wiley & Sons, Inc., Hoboken, New Jersey
Published simultaneously in Canada

For general information about our other products and services, please contact our Customer Care Department within the United States at (800) 762-2974, outside the United States at (317) 572-3993 or fax (317) 572-4002.

Wiley publishes in a variety of print and electronic formats and by print-on-demand. Some material included with standard print versions of this book may not be included in e-books or in print-on-demand. If this book refers to media such as a CD or DVD that is not included in the version you purchased, you may download this material at http://booksupport.wiley.com. For more information about Wiley products, visit www.wiley.com.

Library of Congress Cataloging-in-Publication Data:

Names: Sheridan, Marcus, author.
Title: They ask you answer : a revolutionary approach to inbound sales, content marketing, and today's digital consumer / Marcus Sheridan; foreword by Krista Kotrla.
Description: Hoboken : Wiley, 2017. | Includes index.
Identifiers: LCCN 2016042783 | ISBN 9781119312970 (hardback)
Subjects: LCSH: Marketing. | Sales promotion. | BISAC: BUSINESS & ECONOMICS / Marketing / General.
Classification: LCC HF5415 .S44124 2017 | DDC 658.8–dc23 LC record available at https://lccn.loc.gov/2016042783

Cover design: Paul McCarthy
Cover image: © Alex Belomlinsky/Getty Images, Inc.

Printed in the United States of America

10 9 8 7 6 5 4 3 2

Contents

Foreword

I'm just a construction worker, but when I had a plan and we were working together, we could build a skyscraper. Now you're Master Builders, just imagine what could happen if you did that. You could save the universe.

—Emmet Brickowoski, *The Lego Movie*

Back in 2010 I discovered something surprising. It turns out that it's possible for an average person to save a struggling business and inspire a major culture change throughout an organization. This book is about how.

How is that possible if you're not the CEO? How do you do it if you work remotely, like more than 1,000 miles away from headquarters? What if you are the youngest person on the management team? And a woman just returning from maternity leave? Do you have to mandate it or is it possible to inspire that sort of change?

How does an average person cut budgets, bring in more sales, shorten the buying cycle, increase profits, get other people to market for you, improve employee engagement, *and* dramatically grow the business with a simple four-word strategy? Impossible, you say. Or is it?

What if I told you that it is *very* possible because that's exactly what happened.

Let me share with you a little bit about my journey.

The truth is I couldn't have accomplished any of those things without the help of the ideas, stories, and strategies shared throughout this book with Marcus Sheridan as my guide. Here's how it began. . . .

It started with an urgent problem. Sales were down. *Way* down. So much so that the company was shrinking. Budgets were dramatically cut, product lines were being abandoned, and team members who were dear friends were let go. It was devastating.

On top of that, the industry as we knew it was changing and buyers were increasingly more difficult to reach. E-mails weren't getting through. Trade shows had half the number of attendees. Mailers weren't bringing in any calls. And don't even get me started on fax blasting (can you even believe there was an era when that worked?). To top it all off, somehow even the smallest of our competitors were showing up higher in online search rankings.

Where had all the buyers gone? How were we going to grow with all this stacked against us?

And who was I to think that I could do anything about it?

At that time, I was the marketing manager at Block Imaging, a B2B that buys, sells, and refurbishes used medical imaging equipment; everything from MRI and CT scanners to digital X-ray equipment. Pretty unique niche, right?

It bothered me that we were a worldwide business and yet only 5 percent of our sales were attributed to online inquiries. This became the single statistic that I set out to change *immediately*.

This focus led me to discover a concept commonly referred to as "inbound" or "content" marketing. I was quickly convinced that this was the answer to our most urgent problem. So we signed up for the software and it was going to be a game changer. Marketing automation and blogging were going to change everything, right?

I was wrong.

We needed more than just software. We needed information worth sharing. And we needed a lot of it.

So I set out to connect with people in other departments to collect information worth posting and sharing. How hard could that be?

As enthusiastic as everyone was, here's the gist of how most of those conversations went: "Krista, this all sounds very exciting and I cannot wait to see what *you* do with it. Because I'm in sales, I'm going to go back to selling now. Good luck with your marketing thingy."

New hurdle. Buy-in.

I spent the next six months trying to get buy-in and participation. I gave presentations, offered workshops, invited senior sales leaders to attend social selling conferences with me, unveiled scary statistics as often as

I could. Even after all of that effort, the best traction I could get was about two blog posts a month. And I was sad. Sad because I knew the information we were posting was more brand-centric than customer-centric. Sad because it was taking so much effort to produce sub-par content. Sad because we were running out of time to do this half-assed.

So that's when I made the call. It was the call that would change everything.

I needed reinforcements and knew just the person for the challenge.

Marcus Sheridan had been on this exact same journey of saving a struggling small business with inbound marketing. Even better, he had figured out the most simple and compelling strategy imaginable that resulted in millions of dollars in sales: They Ask, You Answer. His story and examples were just what the Block Imaging team needed to hear. And they needed to hear it from him directly.

It was one of the most important phone calls in my life.

"Marcus, you don't know me or my company yet but you're my guy. I need you to come help me convince the entire Block Imaging team that going all in with inbound is urgent, important, and that with their participation, it is going to be the very best thing that ever happened to our business."

As a result, we began co-designing a two-day workshop to teach, inspire, and jump-start a new culture of inbound companywide. Everyone from sales, engineering, leadership, human resources, administration, project management, and general counsel and the entire accounting team were there.

Did it work?

Without a doubt. What I had just spent the entire previous year trying to rally people around, Marcus accomplished companywide in less than six hours.

He simplified the complex.

Everyone understood.

Everyone bought in.

That day marked a new era for our little organization. We now saw ourselves as teachers, and understood that if we just listened well, and were willing to answer, things would turn around.

We left that two-day event with 700 blog ideas and inspired content generators in every department. More important, we had a unified team with a clear plan for writing a better future, both for the organization and for ourselves. Sharing information and empowering buyers became embedded in our culture.

As a result, we have gone from 5 percent of sales attributed to Web leads to 40 percent of sales from Web leads. In those first two years alone, we could directly tie more than $9 *million* in sales to inbound website leads.

It feels like we've been given a second chance at life.

We are able to serve more people in our industry than ever before with less stress. We have more time and energy for our families and friends. We have fun instead of fear and frustration. We have hope instead of helplessness. We are proactive instead of reactive. We have a mission instead of a position.

This is why we are so excited that Marcus is now sharing his wisdom in this book so that others like me may be inspired and equipped to lead this same type of transformation in their own organizations. Because it is time.

It is time to disrupt the status quo and lead change. It is time to grow an organization that you can be proud of and that buyers trust. It is time to inspire growth in meaningful ways while protecting time and space for the ones you love most. It won't be easy, but with this book you will surely push through the challenges faster and I guarantee it will be worth it.

—Krista Kotrla, CMO, Block Imaging

A Very Different Way of Looking at Business, Marketing, and Trust

If I asked you, "Who is the most trusted voice in your industry?" how would you respond?

Surprisingly, in most industries, such a person or company doesn't even exist. In the following pages, if you truly apply what is taught herein, you'll discover exactly how *you* can become that voice.

1

The Fall

I could feel the anxiety and sense of hopelessness start to overcome me. Like every night at this time, driving home from a long day of work, I dialed my phone and waited for the bank's automated system to tell me what our company's checking account balance was. With heart racing, the response was not surprising.

Overdrawn.

But why was I even checking at this point? Our company bank account had been overdrawn for the past two weeks.

For some reason, though, I still dialed that stupid number, and held out a faint hope that we were in a better situation than what reality demonstrated.

After hanging up the phone and feeling the weight of the world on my shoulders, I started to cry.

I was thirty-one years old. My business was a failure. My family life was suffering. And for a guy who sees himself as a problem solver, I was out of answers.

And so the tears kept flowing, knowing that when I arrived home in a few minutes, my wife Nikki would likely not even ask me the standard question, "So how was work today?"

You see, some questions in life are better off not being asked. My wife understood that. She'd gotten used to seeing the stress in my eyes and the worry in my countenance. The pain was self-evident.

Such was the life of a pool guy in January 2009. . . .

How I Became a "Pool Guy"

Upon graduating from West Virginia University in 2001, my plan was simple: Get an interview and get a job.

By this point in my life, I was already married and had my first child, Danielle (eventually, we'd have four children).

Initially, my plan worked out. I identified a company that I thought would be a great fit, got an interview, and was offered the job immediately. Nikki and I loaded our daughter in the car seat, along with the few belongings we owned in a U-Haul, and headed off to live near Washington, D.C., as I would work in the northern Virginia town of Vienna.

Unfortunately, it didn't take long for me to realize I wasn't thrilled about my new job. To make matters worse, my wife hated the D.C. traffic. So before we entrenched ourselves too deeply, we left D.C. and headed back to the area where we grew up—the "Northern Neck" of Virginia—in order to regroup and figure out what our next step would be.

It was during this time that two of my good friends, Jim Spiess and Jason Hughes, had just started a swimming pool company—River Pools and Spas—and were in the process of opening a small retail store (selling hot tubs, swimming pool supplies, and so on) in the quaint town of Warsaw, Virginia.

Knowing they needed someone to run the retail location while they installed aboveground and inground swimming pools for customers, Jim and Jason asked me if I'd consider managing the store. My response should give you a good feel for where my mind was at the time:

"Sure, I'm happy to help you guys get going until I find out where I'll be working next"—a statement that makes me chuckle to this day.

You see, no one ever says, "I want to be a pool guy when I grow up."

I certainly never saw myself with this title when I was younger, or when I graduated college. But life is a funny thing.

As soon as I started at River Pools, I quickly realized I didn't know much about the industry. Simply "knowing how to swim" wasn't going to help me sell hot tubs, pool chemicals, and the like. So I did what I always do: I learned. I read. I studied. And I dug deep into the industry.

I didn't know how long I was going to be a pool guy, but I did know I didn't want to look dumb in front of customers.

Before long, I started to know a lot about pools and spas. In fact, when Jim and Jason would come into the store, I would quiz them on hot tub brands, distinguishing features, key components, and other subjects. It didn't take them long to realize I suddenly knew a *lot* about the stuff we sold. Customers, too, could see that if they had a question, I generally had an answer. And if I didn't have it, it would bother me so much that I'd assuredly study it so as to better respond on the next occasion.

It was for this reason that Jim and Jason believed I would be the ideal third partner in the business, asking me at the six-month mark if I would join their team for good.

Having no idea about the effect this invitation would have on my life, I simply responded, "Yes."

That was the year 2001.

2001–2008: The False Economy

Growing a business is never an easy thing to do. It doesn't matter the field, or the industry, or the area—it isn't easy.

Nor was it easy in the early years of River Pools and Spas.

There were victories, and there were defeats.

There were many good days and many bad ones as well.

But one thing is for sure—the economy of the United States during these years, specifically the housing market—made it so anyone in the home improvement industry could grow a business and make a decent living, even if they weren't particularly good at what they did.

For River Pools and Spas, the strong economy meant that home values were bloating to ridiculous levels, which therefore enabled almost anyone (if you had a heartbeat, you qualified) to get a second mortgage or a home equity line.

In other words, for the first seven and a half years of the 2000s, *anyone* could get a loan for a swimming pool.

If you (the pool guy) could sell it, they (the homeowner) would find someone to give them the money for it.

Looking back, it doesn't speak too highly of our country's economic system, but it was what it was. And everyone was a part of it, present party included.

2008: The Wheels Start to Fall Off

2008 started off with so much promise. Our company had been through more than our share of ups and downs, and I was invigorated with the prospect of having a banner year. Finally, it looked like we were going to turn the corner and generate sufficient revenue to go into the off season with enough savings in the bank (in Virginia, the main sales season for swimming pool companies is March–September).

By mid-summer of that year, sales were higher than they'd ever been. I can remember looking at the calendar thinking, "Wow, we have two months' worth of pools sold that need to be installed, this is amazing!"

But then, like a sudden earthquake that no one is prepared for, in September of that year, our country's economic system collapsed.

Lehman Brothers went belly up.

The Dow crashed.

John McCain and Barack Obama were on the campaign trail debating what should be done with the failing banks.

It was a chain reaction that seemed to grow worse and worse every day.

In fact, within forty-eight hours of the Dow's crash, we at River Pools and Spas had five customers who had put down deposits to get a pool installed during the winter months essentially tell us, "We're too worried about the economy and cannot move forward with our swimming pool project."

With the average pool installation cost being in the $50,000 range, this equated to roughly $250,000 in losses, all within forty-eight hours.

To say it was a huge blow would be an understatement.

Over the coming months, things went from bad to worse. Our savings, and then our credit, were completely depleted.

By December 2008, we had to tell our employees to stay at home because there was no work to be done.

By January 2009, our business checking account was overdrawn.

Things got so bad that my business partners and I met with multiple business consultants, only to be told, for all intents and purposes, that it was the end of the road for River Pools and Spas—it was time to file bankruptcy.

This pill was a difficult one to swallow. We had given that little swimming pool company everything we had over the previous eight years, and now we were going to not only lose it, but also our homes, our credit, and our foreseeable financial future.

And so there I was, crying in my car that late night in January 2009—account overdrawn, employees sitting at home, and staring bankruptcy square in the face.

No doubt, it was a dark and difficult time in my life.

2

A Massive Buying Shift and the Blur between Sales and Marketing

Before we move on with the fall, and ultimately the rise, of River Pools and Spas, it's critical we address a couple of fundamental truths that, unless understood and embraced, will prevent you from getting anything out of this book whatsoever.

The first is this: *Consumer buying patterns have gone through a monumental shift over the past decade.*

Specifically, the line between "sales" and "marketing" has been completely blurred, if not totally erased.

Multiple recent studies have shown one specific eye-popping statistic:

Today, on average, *70 percent of the buying decision is made* before *a prospect talks to the company*.

Yep, 70 percent.

In other words, before the sales pro ever enters the fray, 70 percent of the buying decision has already been made by the consumer.

And if you're thinking this is a Business-to-Consumer (B2C) study, you're wrong. In fact, originally, this was a Business-to-Business (B2B) study.

Simply put, the 70 percent number resonates across the board regardless of business type, size, location, and so on.

So let's take a minute to analyze what this all means.

If we went back a decade or so, and asked what percentage of the buying decision was made before someone actually talked to the company, what do you think the number would have been?

Most folks would estimate between 20 and 30 percent, as would I.

So if we go with this number and were at 20–30 percent a decade ago, yet find ourselves at 70 percent today, what's the number going to be during the next decade?

Eighty percent?

Ninety percent?

One hundred percent??

Furthermore, let's swallow an even greater pill, one that is weighing on businesses and brands all over the globe:

If this shift is true, which department of your organization has a greater impact on the actual sale? Is it the sales department or the marketing department?

Yep, marketing.

Notwithstanding, generally speaking, when a company is in financial trouble, which is the first department that gets laid off?

Once again, marketing.

And, when a company is looking to grow the business, which is the first to get hired?

Sales.

So the question is, *Why are we doing it this way?*

Because, as I'm sure you'd agree, we've been doing it this way for well over a hundred years.

Sales, in the past, was the driver.

Marketing was the expense.

But no longer are we able to say this.

And no longer can businesses and brands continue to do things the way they've always been done. In fact, as we are thrust into the digital age, it's the ones who aren't doing business as it has always been done who are experiencing the greatest success.

Again and again, as we look around the marketplace, businesses and brands are breaking the rules and defying industry norms to create new rules of doing business.

Zappos did this when they said consumers could ship their shoes back at no cost. At the time, their competitors scoffed. Today, they're all following suit.

Zappos changed the rules.

CarMax, a company we discuss more later in this book, revolutionized the used car industry.

How did they do it? As you'll learn, they simply listened to what consumers wanted … and acted upon it, regardless of whether those in their industry thought it possible or not.

Again, CarMax changed the rules.

The list of examples could go on and on, but the commonality between these companies would remain the same.

They clearly understood consumers had changed, and they knew they had to react or get left behind.

The simple fact is, sales and marketing will never be the same, and will only get more and more blurred over time.

And anything that you and I think must be sold face to face will eventually be sold online.

Scary?

Yeah, I guess you could see it that way. Or, you could see it as a major opportunity, just as so many business have done, while experiencing extraordinary results.

Case in point: In 2015, my swimming pool company sold multiple swimming pools that were more than $100,000 . . . *before* we ever set foot in the customer's home.

Had you told me this was possible just five years ago, I would have laughed in your face.

Today, I realize I was naïve. In fact, I'm not sure any of us fathom just how much consumerism and buyer patterns are going to change in the coming years.

But this much I know: If you adhere to what you read in the following pages, you'll at least be prepared for what comes next, whatever that may be.

3

This Book Won't Work for You If . . .

As mentioned in the previous chapter, there are two things that will dramatically affect whether or not this book has a positive effect on you and your business.

The first, which we just discussed, is the shift in consumer buying patterns and how it has affected sales and marketing as we know it. If you do not believe there is a change in the way consumers behave, there really is no reason to continue reading at this point.

The second element that will affect what you get out of this book is much more personal, and it comes down to a specific mind-set.

You see, as I travel the world and discuss the future of sales and marketing and what businesses must do to be prepared for said future, I find two types of people—two types you've likely also seen time and time again.

The first person (or business), when they hear a new idea, suggestion, or business strategy, responds with:

"Sure, I can see how that's possible."

"I think we might be able to apply that to our business."

"I could see how that would be used within our industry."

And the second, as you may have guessed, is the opposite of the first.

"Nope. Won't work."

"Couldn't be done."

"That's not how our customers buy in our industry."

And on and on.

For the latter, the reason for such a mind-set is simple, and it comes down to one somewhat comical (and sad) belief:

"But you see, Marcus, the stuff you're talking about here may have worked for you and your swimming pool businesses, but at my company, *we're different.*"

Ahh yes, the "we're different" phenomenon.

Funny thing is, I've polled live audiences all over the world, asking thousands of people this one simple question:

"How many of you, by a show of hands, believe your business is quite different than the rest of those in the room?"

And what do you think the results of this question are?

If you guessed 100 percent, you're right.

Everyone thinks their business is different.

Everyone.

Oddly, no one ever says, "Actually, Marcus, we're just like that company over there. . . ."

If one looks at the psychology of this response, the reason why 100 percent of people truly believe their business is different is because they want to feel *special.*

Whether we want to admit it to ourselves or not, this need to feel special runs deep in the world of business.

But, that's the thing. *We're not special,* at least in the most fundamental sort of the word. Case in point: When I was busy leading the life of a pool guy, my business and sales success were, ultimately, built on one thing: *consumer (buyer) trust.*

Then, after I moved on from being full time with River Pools and Spas (to become what is today a silent partner) and started my sales and marketing company, the Sales Lion, once again, I found my business and sales success was built on that same factor: trust.

Fact is, *every* business has a single tie that binds them all together when it comes to consumers and buyers, and that is trust. And the companies that embrace this reality, and let go of the obsession that "we're different" and instead focus on the fact that they are fundamentally the same, that's when great things are brought to pass.

To further make this point, my consulting company, the Sales Lion, has worked with businesses and brands all over the world to help them overcome their digital sales and marketing problems. More than half of these organizations have been B2B. Many have been serviced based. But for each one of them, the big picture doesn't change. We obsess over gaining consumer trust, no matter what title the person has on the other end. In fact, you'll see many of their case studies throughout this book.

So this is my challenge to you: This book will, certainly at times, challenge the way you have done business in your space or industry. When this occurs, don't push aside what is being suggested and automatically dismiss its merits. Instead, ask yourself the simple question, "But is it possible?"

If you do, I can promise you the information found within these pages will have a dramatic impact on your business, and maybe even your life.

So whether you're B2B or B2C, local or national, a service or a product, or whether you're big or small: don't put yourself in the "different" corner.

Bring it back to the basics. Bring it back to trust.

That's the business we're all in.

4

The Discovery
of They Ask,
You Answer

So there we were, on the brink of financial ruin.

If we were going to save the company, we needed a miracle, and it had better occur fast. Unless we found a way to garner more leads and sales than we'd ever had, even though there were fewer potential buyers (because of the economy) than ever before, we were going to go out of business within a matter of months.

Despite this crushing weight, I found myself having moments of reflection about the state of business and economics in general. I believed that times were changing. The way people were buying, shopping, and consuming was dramatically different than it had been just a few years before. All I had to do was look in the mirror to see this change.

I was now turning to the Internet for *everything*. If I had a question, I went to Google and asked. No longer did I need to be an uninformed consumer for anything. Now I had all the knowledge I needed at my fingertips to become an expert at anything I wanted to master. If I wanted to find a product or company reviews, tips, tricks, or anything else—it was all there. It was almost as if every consumer was becoming his own salesperson and subject matter expert.

They were fascinating times indeed, and for me personally. Despite all the stress I was under, I could not stop thinking about the digital opportunities that seemed to be available to any and every business who was but willing to notice.

It was clear as day to me that the Internet was going to change the world and dominate our lives way beyond what I could even fathom. Over the previous years, I'd sensed this stronger and stronger and stronger. No longer was the "old-school" way of advertising working.

In the past, we had tried everything to generate leads at River Pools— TV, radio, newspaper, the Yellow Pages—you name it. Every year we'd spend hundreds and thousands of dollars on these media. And every year their efficacy was becoming less and less.

Seeing this changing of the guard, and knowing things would never go back to the way they were, I knew I had to do something about this problem—and do it quickly.

If my business partners and I were going to save the company, it was time to get our arms around this whole Internet thing and discover how it could save River Pools and Spas from bankruptcy.

So I threw myself in.

Every extra minute of the day I had, I started reading about how to leverage the Internet to grow our business. And as I read articles and watched educational videos (the majority of which I learned on the site www.HubSpot.com), I started to encounter certain phrases popping up, all of which were quite new to me:

- Inbound marketing
- Content marketing
- Social media marketing
- Digital marketing
- Blogging
- And many others

They were fancy words. And they were defined by a whole lot of marketing-speak that was frankly above this pool guy's head. But, if I may be completely transparent here, I think that's what saved me. I didn't view the Internet from an MBA's standpoint. I didn't have years of formal business, sales, or marketing education. Rather, I saw it from a consumer's mind-set.

"Inbound Marketing," as I understood it, was simply the process of attracting (instead of chasing) customers.

And "Content Marketing," was simply the act of teaching and problem-solving so as to earn buyer trust.

This basic way of thinking, in hindsight, was a massive advantage.

And to me, as I read all of these fancy words, suggestions, and strategies, it all came back to one core thought:

Marcus, just answer people's questions.

Okay, I thought, *I can do that.*

After all, that's really what I am at heart: a teacher.

And so all we had to do as a company was become a teacher of fiberglass swimming pools. Once we came to this realization, our company motto took a dramatic shift.

Little did I know that this shift, and the new motto, would go on to affect businesses all over the world.

But it did. And it still does every day.

And as you've likely guessed, the motto was:

"They Ask, You Answer."

5 | "They Ask, You Answer" Defined

What is They Ask, You Answer?

More than anything, it's a *business philosophy*.

It's an approach to communication, company culture, and the way we sell as a business.

They Ask, You Answer starts with an obsession: What is my customer thinking?

And when I say "obsession," I really mean that, and it extends past "What are they thinking?" to "What are they searching, asking, feeling, and fearing?"

Some companies think they understand these questions, but the fact is most do not.

And having a set of defined "buyer personas," at least the way many are defined, doesn't count as sufficient either.

When an organization embraces They Ask, You Answer, they believe it's their duty to be the teacher, the go-to source within their particular industry. One that's not afraid to answer any and every question the prospect or customer may have. For them, it's a moral obligation to do this, regardless of whether the question is perceived as good, bad, or even ugly.

But not only are they willing to address these things better than anyone in their space, they also allow it to dictate the direction of their business as the future unfolds. Because they are so keenly in tune with what the marketplace is thinking, feeling, and asking, they see where their business model needs to go, evolve, and head toward.

Throughout the remainder of this book, we cover—extensively—this philosophy of They Ask, You Answer. You're going to not only see its dramatic impact on River Pools and Spas, but you're also going to watch its impact on multiple companies from various industries (B2B and B2C) around the world. And not only that, but you're going to see how this philosophy goes well beyond the scope of "Internet marketing" and transcends every element of your business philosophy. From online marketing and face-to-face selling to company branding—this is a way of doing business that could revolutionize everything about your company, your culture, and your bottom line.

In part 1 of the book, we look at They Ask, You Answer and its impact on your digital marketing efforts. In particular, we will be focusing on how it guides a company's "inbound" or "content" marketing efforts. (For the sake of ease, these words are used interchangeably throughout the rest of this book.)

In part 2, we discuss how They Ask, You Answer affects the sales side of the business—from the way you sell, to your sales culture, and also the way sales departments are set up in general.

Next, in part 3, we discuss implementation of this methodology in your business, showing you the *who, what, when, where, why,* and *how* to make it all work.

And then finally, in part 4 of the book, we take some of the commonly asked questions most organizations ask upon hearing this approach to business, and answer each one so as to resolve any concerns and fill in any gaps you may still have—with the hope it will be the finishing touch to taking your business and brand—regardless of type, size, and so on—to a place of strength for years and years to come.

6 | Brainstorming the Questions You Are Asked Every Day

Now that I'd discovered the core philosophy we'd be adhering to as we moved forward with River Pools and Spas, it was time to act.

My first action was simple: I sat down at my kitchen table late one night and brainstormed all the questions I'd received about fiberglass swimming pools over the previous nine years.

As you might imagine, the writing was fast and furious. After all, I sold swimming pools for a living. I heard questions from prospects and customers all day long, so the idea of simply recalling these questions was by no means difficult. After about thirty minutes, I had more than a hundred questions listed on the paper.

Wow.

What happened next is where things became very interesting. I took these questions I listed and over the coming months, late at night when everyone in my house was asleep. I (along with my two business partners) would write articles or make videos answering each of them. Most of these articles were published to our website as blog articles, with the question itself becoming the title of the post. The videos were uploaded to YouTube and also placed on the website.

For me, this whole process became somewhat of a religion. If I was on a sales appointment, as soon as the prospect would ask me a question my immediate thought was, *Have I answered that on our website yet?*

And remember, I'm not talking here about one- or two-sentence answers to questions. I'm talking about really answering the question, including deep explanations while approaching each with a "teacher's" mentality—without bias and trying only to educate the reader.

At the time, I had no idea this little brainstorming activity and corresponding content production would end up being something I'd use to help guide numerous other sales and marketing teams do for their own brands and organizations. I never could have imagined that during the coming years so many other businesses around the globe would embrace their own forms of They Ask, You Answer.

The fact is, every industry has hundreds of questions about what prospects and customers want to know when they're making a buying decision. Whether it's B2B or B2C, everyone wants to feel like they've made an informed buying decision, and they certainly don't want to make any mistakes.

The irony is that every industry has hundreds of buyer-based questions. It is the sad reality that most company websites don't even address more than a few dozen of these questions.

It's a digital paradox of sorts.

As consumers, we expect to be fed *great* information.

As businesses, we like to talk about ourselves and therefore don't focus on what our prospects and customers are thinking about, worrying about, and asking about.

The whole thing is contrary to the very nature of that which we call "building trust."

This brings us to the first major step of They Ask, You Answer.

Putting It Into Action

Have a Brainstorm Session

Brainstorm every question you've ever been asked by a prospect or customer. Focus on his or her fears, issues, concerns, and worries. State them on paper exactly as the consumer would ask (or search) them, not the way you (as the business) would state them. Once you've completed this list, you have the foundation for your entire digital marketing editorial calendar—be it articles, videos, and so on—to put on your company website.

Note: If you struggle coming up with these questions, there's a frank reason why: you've lost touch with your ideal customer or client. If this is the case, it's time to get with your sales team, customer service team, and everyone else, and relearn what your ideal customer wants to know to be able to make an informed buying decision.

7 | The Ostrich Marketing Strategy

Before we dive into They Ask, You Answer, it's important to note here another sales and marketing strategy, one that you likely weren't taught in business school but is commonplace around the world today and is the literal opposite of They Ask, You Answer: I call it "ostrich marketing."

Why is it called ostrich marketing? Look at it this way: An ostrich, when it has a problem, does what?

It buries its head in the sand (which is a myth, but we'll go with it anyway).

And why does it bury its head in the sand?

Because it thinks the problem will go away.

But does the problem ever go away? Of course, the answer is no.

Now, you're probably wondering what an ostrich has to do with you, your business, and the way you communicate online and offline.

Look at it this way: How many times have you been asked a question from a prospect or customer and thought to yourself, *We better not address that issue on our website. Let's just wait until we are talking face to face with the prospect and then bring it up.*

My guess is this has happened to you many times. And if you can't think of an example, you will. As you read the following pages, you'll find many examples of subjects you have very likely shied away from talking about on your website simply because you *thought* it would put you at a disadvantage, and you wanted to be able to control the conversation.

27

But therein lies the entire problem with ostrich marketing: consumers (you and I) don't like it. To put it more bluntly, we abhor it.

Here are the facts about ostrich marketing (or ignoring the questions of your prospects and customers):

- In our digital era, the ostrich does not win.
- The ostrich does not engender trust.
- The ostrich does not get the phone call, the store visit, or the online purchase.
- The ostrich does not get anyone filling out contact forms on his or her website.

The solution? Don't be the ostrich. Do whatever it takes to earn their trust.

Embrace They Ask, You Answer.

8

The CarMax Effect

To truly understand They Ask, You Answer, you must see that it goes well beyond the scope of "Let's produce articles and videos on our website to answer customer questions."

In fact, as previously mentioned, They Ask, You Answer is a *business philosophy*.

It's the willingness to be so focused on and obsessed with consumer questions, wants, desires, and needs that you're willing to change and evolve your entire business model around these elements.

To understand this on a deeper level, let's talk about a subject that, without fail, draws a *unique* emotion from consumers: *buying a used car.*

When you hear the phrase "buy a used car" or "used car salesperson," what is the emotion you experience? What words come to mind?

Sleazy?

Salesy?

High pressure?

The list goes on and on. What's even more interesting is that consumers all over the world share these same negative thoughts. Having spoken in multiple continents and to multiple cultures, I can assure you that no one ever shouts, "Trustworthy!" when I ask this question.

This phenomena begs the question: How did the used car industry get to this point?

What happened to make so many consumers around the world lose trust in an entire industry?

To answer this question, let's look at the specifics.

If you were going to go out and buy a used car today, what would be some of your (potential) fears?

Across hundreds of global audiences, the answers are almost always the same:

1. You don't want to buy a lemon. (You don't want a car with a bunch of problems, false mileage, bad history, and so on.)
2. You don't want to have to haggle with the salesperson (high-pressure sales tactics, back and forth with the sales manager, and so on).
3. You want to make sure you're getting a good value and not getting ripped off.
4. You don't want to buy the car and then find out it's the wrong vehicle for you (a.k.a.: buyer's remorse).

For years, consumers have had these fears when buying a used car, but few companies cared about addressing them. That is, until CarMax came around.

The Beginnings of CarMax and a New Way to Sell

The story of CarMax is a powerful one. Based out of Richmond, Virginia, this company went from being doubted by an entire industry of peers to becoming what is today the largest retailer of used vehicles in the United States. Now, you may not think that this fact in and of itself is profound until you analyze what they did to reach the pinnacle of their industry.

Essentially, CarMax did two things other used car companies weren't willing (at least at the time) to do:

1. Admit their industry had a problem (no consumer trust).
2. Ask themselves what it would take to earn that trust back.

You see, most businesses and brands never like to admit there is anything wrong with their company, industry, or the way business is generally done. Instead, much like the ostrich, they simply convince themselves it's business as usual—ultimately ignoring needed change.

But CarMax was the antithesis of the "business as usual" paradigm.

Specifically, they did what almost no one else was willing to do.

The first action they took to garner trust back from consumers was to attack the issue of "I don't want to deal with the salesperson" head-on by offering what they referred to as "no-haggle pricing." In other words, with no haggle pricing, consumers were given one listed price for the vehicles, nothing more, nothing less.

For example, if you walk into a CarMax today and write a check for $29,999 on a car that's listed for $30,000—they will not sell you the vehicle unless you come up with another dollar.

Some might argue this hurts CarMax's ability to create a sense of urgency and scarcity with the buyer, but the opposite is true. Consumers love the fact they have but one number (price) to focus on, ultimately lowering their anxiety levels while phenomenally boosting trust for the brand in the process.

But CarMax didn't stop there. Beyond offering one price, they set up their sales team on a flat-rate, one- commission structure as well—meaning whether they sold the most expensive or the least expensive car on the lot, they would get the same commission.

As you might imagine, by doing this, CarMax has eliminated a salesperson's need to think about themselves (wanting a higher commission) over the consumer (getting the right vehicle based on need)—ultimately leading to dramatically more trust during the buying process because the customer believes the company, and the salesperson, have their best interest at heart.

Despite the fact that competitors originally scorned this sales philosophy at CarMax, the end result was groundbreaking, and in the process, CarMax was able to overcome the issue of salesperson distrust—the biggest plague facing their entire industry.

But CarMax continued to take things further. They recognized other fears consumers had and again sought to eliminate them—regardless of the way it had previously been done in the industry.

Their next groundbreaking move came when they started offering a five-day money-back guarantee to customers. In other words, if you bought a car from CarMax and realized during that first week the vehicle was not a good fit for you (for whatever reason), they'd take the car back.

At the time of offering this, the idea of a five-day money-back guarantee was, for most car dealers, preposterous.

In fact, to this day, in many countries the idea is still foreign and unheard of.

But because CarMax was building a consumer-centric business philosophy (that permeated every facet of their company), they simply didn't care whether other companies were or were not offering this type of guarantee.

And the end result?

Once again they were able to overcome, and practically eliminate, one of the biggest fears in buying a used car: buyer's remorse.

Another groundbreaking CarMax move was turning their attention to quality control. Instead of following the traditional pattern of selling vehicles with previous issues or problems in an effort to net huge profits, they took the necessary steps to ensure they could limit these issues to the best of their ability.

To give you a sense of this, if you walk into a CarMax as a consumer today, one of the first questions they are going to ask you is "Are you familiar with the process by which our vehicles qualify to be sold on our lot?"

Upon asking this, their next action is a critical one of trust building in that they take the time to physically show you the intensive inspection process their cars have to go through in order to meet their vehicle standards. Furthermore, they *want* you to see how the majority (roughly 66 percent) of the vehicles they buy (in trade-ins or straight from consumers) never make it to the sales lot.

You have likely heard auto dealers brag on their commercials or websites about their "ninety-point (or thereabouts) inspection process" to ensure vehicle quality. Although CarMax may not have started this trend, they were certainly one of the first to physically *show* each of these inspection points to their potential customers.

After all, seeing is believing.

You see, in business, just talking about something isn't enough. If you truly want to overcome concerns and make your point real, you need to show it. You must teach it. And you certainly must be willing to address it.

In our digital and visual world, one thing is certain:

If you don't *show* it, it doesn't exist.

"We have great customer service" is likely said by everyone else in your industry. And if everyone is saying it, you can be assured it means nothing to the consumer—that is, again, until you show it.

The same goes for every other overused business adjective that typically litters business copy, slogans, and website messaging.

CarMax proved this point by physically showing customers their vehicle inspection system. And furthermore, they were one of the first brands to add a CarFax vehicle history report as a standard with all their vehicles—allowing the prospective buyer to see the vehicle's history, once again eliminating seeds of doubt and adding further confidence to the buyer.

As you might imagine, between demonstrating their intensive vehicle inspection process and showing the vehicle history report, CarMax was able to overcome a third major consumer fear: *the fear of buying a lemon.*

At this point, CarMax has now eliminated three major fears of buying a used vehicle:

1. Dealing with the salesperson
2. Buyer's remorse
3. Buying a lemon

As mentioned earlier, there is only one more consumer concern left:

4. Not getting ripped off (or wanting to get great value, which is essentially the same thing).

And how did CarMax overcome that fear? Well, the answer is simple: besides listing the Kelley Blue Book value with all their vehicles, they did that which you already read.

And by taking these steps, CarMax allowed the consumer to sense the extreme value. And in this case, it's the value of trust, which is the entire rise or fall of any brand and business.

But imagine for a second that you went back in time fifteen or twenty years and were tasked with speaking to a group of one hundred used car professionals on how to increase sales and revenue with their businesses. Now imagine telling them that the key to their future success would be found by offering no-haggle pricing, a five-day money-back guarantee, an intensive inspection process with the goal of never selling a lemon again, and a way for consumers to trust in the value of the car.

How do you think that audience would have responded to such recommendations?

Yep, they likely would have thrown you out of the room.

And the reason they would have thrown you out is because such rec-ommendations were practically heresy two decades ago.

In fact, there was a time when used car companies laughed at the CarMax business model.

But today, these same companies have now had to change their busi-ness model to match that of CarMax's.

You see, every industry is made up of two groups: those who listen to the consumer and act (They Ask, You Answer), and those who maintain the status quo.

But time and time again, history has shown us that those who listen to the consumer and change their business model—regardless of what others may say—set the standard for their space. They become the rule makers.

And the competition? Well, they become the rule followers.

I hope you can clearly see that the amazing story of CarMax can be applied to any industry—regardless of B2B status, B2C status, size, locality, and so on.

In fact, with many of our clients (spread across multiple industries) at my company, the Sales Lion, we've applied this "CarMax Effect" again and again, often with astounding results.

Simply put, the greatest companies and modern-day rule makers are obsessed with consumer fear, and they allow that fear to dictate their entire business model. And they do this because they know if they are able to eliminate all fears and negative emotions from the buying process, the only emotion left to feel is trust.

And trust, quite frankly, is really what this book (and being in business) is all about.

Uber did this in the transportation space by rating drivers and coming up with dramatically more customer-friendly ways of transportation.

Zappos did this in the clothing space by offering free returns.

The examples go on and on, but the principle remains the same.

Consumers ask for it, smart businesses answer it—and often change history in the process.

I'll share one last story about CarMax, one that would be hard to believe if I hadn't been there myself.

In early 2016, I found myself speaking to a company in Houston, Texas, telling them the story of CarMax. When I was done, the owner of the company stood up in the room and stated:

"I agree with everything Marcus has said. In fact, I once bought a car (a Porsche even!) from CarMax but ended up returning it the first week. Why did I return it? Well, my dog didn't like it and couldn't seem to get comfortable, and that's exactly what I told the company when I returned the vehicle. I didn't believe they'd actually refund my money until I saw a check in the mail for the full amount four days later."

I told you the story was crazy.
But such is the stuff legendary companies are made of.
Well done, CarMax.

Putting It Into Action

Have a Healthy Relationship with Fear

Allow it to guide your business.

The following activity, albeit incredibly simple, can do wonders for your business, so give it a try. I've done this with multiple organizations to produce profound results.

Just as we did with used cars, take a moment to brainstorm every single reason (fear, worry, question, concern) as to why someone would *not* buy from your company. What would hold them back? What would keep them from clicking "buy," swiping their credit card, or writing that big check?

If you do this activity properly (especially if you do it with fellow employees), you should come up with ten to twenty reasons, if not more (sadly, a surprising number of businesses struggle with this one small task, all because they've lost touch with the most important part of their business: what the potential customer is thinking).

Once you've listed each of these fears or reasons for not buying, now comes the critical step:

How many of these issues (fears, worries, concerns, questions, objections, and others) have already been addressed well (a few sentences doesn't count) on your company website?

How many have been addressed within your sales process?

(Seriously, take the time to do this activity. If you don't, you're going to not only miss the whole point, but you'll also miss a chance to discover some very interesting things about your business.)

If you're like the majority of the brands and businesses I've consulted with, when it comes to your website, the answer is almost always between 10 and 20 percent of the issues.

In other words, the majority of companies never take the time to properly address the biggest fears of their buyers (and leave it to the face-to-face part of the sales process to overcome these objections), and it's costing businesses millions of dollars each year.

So the question is, Is it possible for you to address, and even eliminate, all of those issues you wrote down?

Find a way to do this, and you'll likely revolutionize your industry and innovate in ways you previously had not imagined.

But it all starts with an obsession in knowing their objections, and then being willing to do something about it.

This is They Ask, You Answer.

9

The Discovery of
the Big 5

Within a couple of months after commencing They Ask, You Answer on the River Pools and Spas website, I could see that what we were doing was already making a difference.

By publishing four to five pieces of content each week on our site, it seemed like searchers (those people looking for swimming pools) and search engines (Google, Yahoo, and others) were clearly taking notice.

We were getting more Web traffic.

Leads started to increase, many of whom were more educated and qualified because of the content they had read and consumed.

Even a few sales were being made.

Although we weren't breaking the bank, and even though we (and the economy) had a long way to go, there was real progress.

And it was exciting.

After about six months of They Ask, You Answer, I took the time to take a deep dive into our Web analytics in an effort to pick up on any patterns that may have been occurring. Essentially, I wanted to know what was working, what wasn't working, and also the types of content that were getting the most traction and results.

What I discovered was profound.

Basically, there were five types of content subjects (or types of questions) that seemed to move the needle with readers more than anything else, ultimately rendering the greatest amount of traffic, conversions, leads, and sales. These five subjects were as follows:

1. Pricing and Costs
2. Problems
3. Versus and Comparisons
4. Reviews
5. Best in Class

At the time, what I didn't realize was that these five subjects weren't at all specific to the swimming pool industry. Rather, these are the five main subjects consumers and businesses research the most whenever they're getting ready to make a purchasing decision.

As mentioned multiple times already, what I'm explaining here is not a B2B or B2C issue. It's all encompassing, as our studies have shown time and time again.

Over time, once I realized how these five subjects transcend all industries, I dubbed them "the Big 5," and their influence remains as great as it has ever been.

But with the Big 5, there is an interesting phenomenon that occurs between businesses and consumers.

As consumers, we often obsess over these five subjects when considering a purchase.

As businesses, we generally ignore or even hide from these questions, hoping they'll either magically go away or, worst case, willingly address them only when we are face to face with the prospect or buyer.

In other words, we're experiencing a literal paradox of business strategy, while essentially *not* doing unto others as we would have them do unto us.

Although you may be confused about how to understand and implement the Big 5 in your business, the following chapters cover each individually and show you specific ways you can address these five critical subjects, ultimately winning the trust of searchers and search engines alike. . . .

10 | Content Subject 1 Pricing and Costs: *Why We Must Talk about Money*

Have you ever researched online how much something costs?

Assuredly, if you've been alive, you have.

But when you're on a company's website, and there is nothing about the costs of their product or services, what is the emotion you experience?

Frustration, right?

I've asked this question to hundreds and hundreds of audiences, and overwhelmingly, "Frustrated" is the number one response, which is exactly why I've dubbed it the "F-word of the Internet."

But let's analyze this together for a minute.

What gives you the right to be frustrated when you're on a business's website and can't find any cost or price information?

For starters, you're frustrated because you feel like you're wasting your time and not getting the answers you're looking for.

Furthermore, you're thinking to yourself, *I'm the customer! It's my money. And it's my right to know.*

But if we look at this at an even deeper level, you're upset because *you* know that the *business* knows the answer to the question. And because *you* know that *they know* the answer, you now feel like they are *hiding* something from you.

When you're researching a company and their products and services, the moment you feel like anyone is hiding anything from you, all trust is lost.

Let's continue, though, to analyze your online behavior in this moment of frustration at not finding the information you're looking for.

Do you say to yourself, *Well, I'm just going to dig a little deeper on this website and see if I can find the answer?* No, of course you don't do that. In fact, the idea of staying on a website that clearly doesn't have what you're looking for is almost insulting to your Internet intelligence.

Or, do you say to yourself: *Oh, it's okay that this company is not talking about their prices, I'm sure they're a "value"-based business. I'll just call them instead?*

I bet you don't say that either, do you? In the past you may have called them, but today, you don't.

Instead of continuing to dig on their site or calling them directly, today you keep looking. And you do it elsewhere.

And you continue to look until someone answers your original question. And whoever is willing to answer your question first, in most cases, is the one who will get the first phone call or contact. They're also the one who will likely get your business. In other words, they are the one who has earned your trust.

The search behavior just described is consistent for just about any company and culture around the world. As consumers, we expect answers. When we don't get them, we get upset and leave. Our loyalty is to the honest and open teacher focused on *our* problems.

That being said, Do you, right now, on your company site, talk a lot about the cost of your products or services?

If you are like the thousands of others who've heard me ask this question, you are likely starting to experience a little bit of internal strife contemplating why you do or do not discuss pricing on your website. There's maybe even a civil war going on inside your head. What I have found is that fewer than 10 percent of all businesses in the world (not including e-commerce) address pricing and costs on their company website. It doesn't matter whether they are B2B or B2C businesses, or whether they are product or service oriented, only a small percentage ever address the question of pricing and costs.

So the question is, Why?

Why are you (assuming you fall in the 90 percent) not currently discussing cost and price on your website?

Regardless of company or culture, we have found there are three reasons businesses justify not discussing this subject on their website:

1. "Every solution is different. Our prices vary."
2. "If we discuss pricing on our website, our competitors will find out what we charge."
3. "If we show what we charge, we'll scare customers away."

1. Every Solution Is Different

I'm sure this statement is true, but look at it this way: When was the last time you were on a website, couldn't find pricing information, and said to yourself, *Of course they can't talk about pricing, there are simply too many variables.*

If you're anything like most consumers, you frankly don't care that a company's prices vary. In fact, with any common sense, you already know this. You understand they can't be exact, but you do certainly feel the least they could do is give you a sense for what to except and some possible ranges as to where you might be.

As a business, you must ask yourself whether it's possible to discuss this question of variable costs. Could you explain the factors that keep the costs down? Could you explain the elements that push the cost of a project up? Could you help the readers (or viewers, listeners, or other type of customer) understand all the factors that dictate cost within your industry as they're doing their research?

Chances are, if you want to give the potential customer a feel for how pricing works within your industry, as well as how pricing works within your company, you could very likely do it.

2. Our Competitors Will Find Out What We Charge

This one is often the most laughable: Most companies already know exactly, or at least have a very good feel, as to what their competitors charge.

In other words, it's not a big secret.

Everyone knows what everyone else is charging.

It's almost like saying you have a "secret sauce" when in reality everyone knows it's just Thousand Island dressing.

Plus, if you consider this even further, you have to ask yourself why you'd ever let the competition dictate your ability to educate, and ultimately gain the trust of, your ideal customers.

One of these groups takes your business, and the other *is* your business.

3. We'll Scare Customers Away

Think about this one for a second. It's as if you're saying, "If I'm honest, people won't want to do business with me."

But if we look at how *we* behave and what *we* expect as consumers, the thing that actually scares us away is the idea of a company *not* addressing cost and price on their website.

To crystallize this point, imagine you're taking a friend to dinner tonight and you all have decided to try a restaurant you've never been to. Before going, if you're like most people, you're going to research two main things before you walk through their front doors: online reviews (like Yelp) and the restaurant's website.

In this case, the main reason you want to go to their website that you want to look at their menu.

Well, what happens if you go to the menu and you find that it lists items but *not* prices? What do you do?

If you're like most people, you'll not go to that restaurant, not because you couldn't afford to go there, but rather because of the simple fact that they didn't want to show it, which planted seeds of doubt in your mind as the consumer. And as consumers, where there are seeds of doubt, inaction and the inability to make a buying decision almost always occur.

Folks, discussing cost and price is not about affordability, it's about psychology. It's about trust. And believe it or not, every business can do it, as we now explain.

11

How One Article about Money Generated More Than $3,000,000 in Sales

For years in my career as a pool guy, whenever a potential customer would call me, within the first five minutes of a conversation I would almost always hear the same question:

"Marcus, I'm not going to hold you to it, but could you at least give me a feel for how much something like this is going to cost?"

For a long time, that question bothered me as a business owner. I wanted to talk about products, benefits, and features, but the customer wanted to immediately know about pricing.

In hindsight, the fact that I let this bother me so much was foolish. If roles had been reversed, I would have wanted to know the same thing.

In other words, as consumers and buyers, we at least like to have a sense of how much things cost before we spend hours upon hours dedicated to learning about that product, service, company, and so on.

Once I stopped thinking like a business owner and started thinking like the consumer (They Ask, You Answer), I realized one of the most important pieces of content I could produce would be the one that addressed the question, "How much does a fiberglass pool cost?"

So after years of not wanting to address this subject until I was face to face with a prospect, I shifted and wrote the article shown in Figure 11.1 on my company website.

In it, I explain how buying a fiberglass pool was much like buying a car—there were many options, accessories, and so on. I listed each one, offering to the consumer a true sense of the potential scope of a project.

Next, I explained different types of packages we offered as a company: how some buyers wanted a pool in the ground without any patio, landscaping, or other features, and how others were just the opposite–wanting a true "turn-key" installation, complete with patio, fencing, landscaping, and so on.

With each of these, we gave large ranges as to what the buyer might expect to spend, but ultimately, after 1,000+ words of explanation, we said the answer to the question of "How much does it cost?" was "It depends."

How Much Does a Fiberglass Pool Cost?

One of the first questions potential pool owners want to know when they call our company is : **How much does a fiberglass pool cost?** Although this is a very difficult question to answer, I will try to do my best here to explain some general pricing guidelines.

The purchase of a swimming pool is much like the purchase of a vehicle or even a home. With so many options available, price ranges can vary drastically. Just as a Ford F150 can start around 20k with just a basic package, it can quickly cost over 40k once a shopper adds such items as power windows, CD player, all-leather interior, chrome finishes, extended cab, 4-wheel drive, 4 doors versus two, upgraded wheels, dual exhaust, spray-on bedliner, built-in GPS system, etc, etc. Considering that the average American sells or trades in their vehicle

Figure 11.1   How Much Does a Fiberglass Pool Cost? Web article, 2009

What happened next was very, very interesting.

You see, when I wrote this article "How Much Does a Fiberglass Pool Cost?" on our website in 2009, take a guess as to how many other swimming pool builders had addressed this question on their company websites?

If you answered zero, you are correct.

No one did it. Out of the thousands of pool builders around the globe, every single one of them was the ostrich with its head in the sand.

And of course, the reasons why they didn't address it were the same reasons we discussed earlier:

1. Each project is different and therefore costs vary.
2. They didn't want their competitors to see their pricing.
3. They were afraid they'd scare prospects away if they honestly discussed pricing.

But for us at River Pools, the fact that no one had addressed this question meant a blue ocean of opportunity for the business. The marketplace was dying for someone to be open and honest enough to address this question, and so that's exactly what we did.

We saw immediate action on two fronts.

Within days of posting the article on our website, we noticed an increase in qualified, productive conversations with leads who contacted us. Many people commented on how impressed they were to "finally" find a company that was willing to discuss the subject of cost and price.

But with search engines like Google, things got even more interesting. Within forty-eight hours from the time I posted the new page on our site, the article became the first article to pop up any time someone went online and searched anything to do with how much a fiberglass pool cost. In fact, here is a list of keyword phrases for which this article ranked number 1 in Google search engine results, all within days of publishing the post:

- How much does a fiberglass pool cost?
- How much does it cost to install a pool?
- Cost of in-ground swimming pool
- Fiberglass pool cost
- Fiberglass pool pricing
- And on and on

Now, you might say, "Well, that's fine, but website traffic doesn't necessarily equate to money. It takes more than traffic to get a customer."

And if you were thinking this, you're exactly right. What we're discussing here isn't about getting more traffic to your website. Fact is, Web traffic doesn't pay your bills, *sales* do.

Luckily, the tools (in this case HubSpot) we used on our site allowed us to track how people were finding our company and what they were searching for when they found us. So over the course of time, we saw how this one article would send our company more than 1 million new visitors, thousands of whom would eventually become leads and hundreds more who would "request a quote"—all because they originally had searched a phrase that had to do with the cost of a fiberglass swimming pool.

But here is the key question that one must consider: If that article had never been written, would any of those sales appointments have ever occurred? The answer, of course, is no. The prospective buyer (very likely) never would have found us and shown up to our site in the first place—all because we hadn't been willing to address the subject. But in our case, *we were willing to address the question*. And because of this, search engines like Google showed that article (and our website) to thousands and thousands of potential buyers. And because of that, many of these potential buyers were able to say to themselves:

Okay, now I have a much better sense of what would drive the cost of a fiberglass swimming pool up or down. I now know what to expect.

With this education came a feeling of trust, and many visitors eventually filled out a form to get a quote for a swimming pool. Because we're able to track the people who filled out a form (from the cost article) and know which ones bought a swimming pool, we know the value of each one of these customers—a value that can be directly tied to that one article that was written about the cost of a fiberglass pool.

Here is the culminating point: We know that since the time this article was written on our site in 2009, it has made our company more than $3 million in additional sales—revenue we would *not* have gotten had we been an ostrich with our head in the sand.

Think about that: *$3 million in sales* simply because we were willing to explain to prospective customers that the cost of a fiberglass swimming pool depends on several factors. Without exaggeration, this single article saved my business. It saved my home. It saved the homes of my two business partners. It also saved the jobs of all of our employees.

But the funny thing is, we never specifically stated how much a fiberglass pool costs. We simply answered the question the best we could. We were honest. We openly discussed the industry as a whole. And in the process of doing that, my entire business, and ultimately my life, was altered dramatically.

Fellow reader, this is the power of honesty, transparency, and seeing yourself as a teacher. But sadly, most businesses, especially in the B2B space, still don't recognize this massive need to openly discuss the issue of pricing, budgets, money, and related topics on one's website.

As mentioned earlier, I now have a digital sales and marketing agency that helps companies all over the world generate more trust, traffic, leads, and sales. More than 50 percent of these clients are B2B. And with more than 80 percent of all of these clients, the number 1 traffic, lead, and sales-generating content has to do with money, costs, and even salaries (if you're looking to recruit great people, answer their questions about salary).

Remember, it doesn't necessarily matter what you specifically say in terms of the numbers. What matters is that you're willing to teach your prospective customers what would drive the cost up or down and help them get a feel for the marketplace.

Over the years, I've had dozens upon dozens of companies approach me and discuss this matter of pricing, only to tell me how they simply can't discuss numbers on their website because their competition charges so much less than they do. My response is always the same:

"Why is their product or service cheaper?"

Almost always, the response has to do with overseas manufacturers, low quality, customer experience, and so on.

Once again, my retort is always the same:

"Have you bothered to explain these factors well on your company website?"

In almost every industry, consumers make poor buying decisions and purchase the "cheapest" products and services, not because they are solely price motivated, but rather because they don't know any better. They haven't been educated. No one has bothered to truly explain the good, the bad, and the ugly of the industry. And that, once again, is the fault of the business, not the consumer.

Along these same lines, at the Sales Lion any time a client of ours states specific pricing on their site, they inevitably find such a strategy generates better, higher-qualified opportunities. With specific pricing on their site, they spend less time dealing with prospects who never would have been a good fit in the first place and instead focus their energies on educated, ideal-fit prospects who aren't just looking for the cheapest thing, but rather the best value.

My point to you and your business is this: When it comes to money, you cannot be the ostrich with your head in the sand.

You must be willing to address the most important questions—regardless of whether you're a service, product, value driven, and so on.

Remember, it doesn't matter what you and I think—what matters is what consumers think, how they behave, and what they expect.

So the question is, Are you willing to meet their expectations?

Or, would you prefer that the competition be the one who answers the question for them?

Remember, they're going to get their answers from someone, so wouldn't you prefer they get their answers from you?

Putting It Into Action

Focus on Cost, Price, Salary, and So On

At this point, I want to repeat the question we discussed earlier in this chapter:

Based on what you have now read, would it be possible for you to address the question of pricing and costs (or even salary) on your website?

Remember, I'm not suggesting you put a "price list" on your site. Rather, be willing to specifically address the main pricing questions you get. To do this effectively, complete the following activity:

1. List out all the major products and services you sell.
2. Once this list is complete, identify the items and services that generate the most revenue and/or have the most opportunity for you as a company.
3. Now, for each one of these, produce at least one article and video explaining the factors that dictate costs, what the buyer can expect to see in the industry, and where you fall as a company.

4. Place this content on your company website. In fact, we strongly recommend to clients that they have a "pricing" tab on the home pages
   of their websites, and that the content therein funnels visitors to the
   articles and videos that address these core pricing questions.
5. Immediately start using this content throughout your sales process
   (as we discuss later in the book).

12

Case Study 1

High-End B2B Technology Company Generates More Than $8,000,000 in Additional Revenue

Note: As mentioned previously, throughout this book we integrate powerful stories of businesses that have embraced They Ask, You Answer in their own ways to achieve extraordinary results. As is the case with Segue Technologies, you will hear about them embracing strategies that are covered later in the book. When this occurs, you can simply consider it a preview of what is to come in later chapters, as it all will become very clear by the end.

In today's world, few industries are as competitive as technology. In order to stand out in these types of businesses, companies often have to embrace new and creative ways of thinking and doing things, or watch as their business slowly fades away into oblivion only to be replaced by the next guy who had the foresight to embrace the vision of the future.

Segue Technologies is a perfect example of a company that saw the power of great teaching and transparency as a new and more efficient way of doing business, and quickly set out to be the first, and best, to do it in their industry.

About Segue Technologies

Segue Technologies specializes in application development and support services for federal, commercial, and nonprofit companies looking to have their IT challenges solved.

Segue provides custom Web applications, solves data management problems, and supports the evolution of the mobile workforce.

Segue's goal is to help clients customize their IT services in a way that saves them money, improves their performance, and allows them to work more efficiently.

Rather than pushing a one-size-fits-all solution for their clients, Segue customizes solutions based on the specific needs of each of their clients.

Ron Novak, Segue Technologies' executive vice president, discusses the changes Segue has made over the years to their marketing efforts and business model (going from just Business to Government [B2G] to Business to Business [B2B]) as they continue to stay at the forefront of the IT solutions industry.

> "Initially, we started off doing Windows-based desktop development, mostly for procurement software and budgeting software for the Air Force. As technology changed rapidly, we moved to doing Web application development and branched off into doing commercial as well, and then expanded from working with just the Air Force to working with the Marine Corps, Navy, and Army."

For a couple of years, Segue was comfortable growing their business strictly through the Armed Services sectors. However, during a time of government budget cuts, Segue realized (as many did in the B2G space) that in order to continue growing and evolving, they would have to branch out into the commercial space as well. Says Novak:

> "It was almost like an experiment just to see if we could even do commercial work. Fortunately, we ended up landing some pretty large clients. We started working with Sprint, Five Guys, and the United Negro College Fund. We had some good diversification at that point, which allowed us to kind of weather the storm during the government sequestration."

Novak quickly realized that doing business in the commercial space was quite different from doing business in the government space. Rather than using advertising, most of the business they had solicited from the federal government came via word of mouth and attending networking events.

"Before 2008, it was almost exclusively word of mouth, organic growth, and networking events. Doing business in the government space is a lot different than in the commercial world, so a lot of our marketing was just in-person networking and relationship building."

Like many companies, Segue Technologies had a business website, but they hadn't really been utilizing it. Novak realized the value a solid, evolving website and blog could add to the business if they were going to enter the commercial space with any success.

"We were slightly ahead of the curve of the defense contractors in that we actually saw the value in having a good website and having good content. But we really didn't know what good content meant for a long time. Even though we wrote some blogs back then, they were very inconsistent. We were lucky to do one or two a month, and we didn't really have a strategy behind the content we created, as it certainly wasn't close to aligning with They Ask, You Answer."

Although Segue had been taking a little time to try and bolster their website traffic through blogging, they weren't seeing the results they had hoped for.

"We were still growing—we were growing every year, but a lot of that was because of organic growth in our normal customer base. But very rarely did we get new customers coming to our website. We would get interest and maybe some decent leads every once in awhile, but we didn't close many leads from the Web. It was kind of one of those things that you really had to have a good website on the commercial side more than the government side. A lot of organizations in the DOD [Department of Defense] space don't really think that your website is that important, and they still don't. It's still kind of an antiquated world in many ways, so I viewed it as a huge opportunity to differentiate ourselves from other competitors in our space and start to establish ourselves as thought leaders in our industry."

Novak was attending an event in the summer of 2012 when he heard me discuss the power of content, transparency, and They Ask, You Answer.

"It was during Marcus's presentation that I had kind of a 'light-bulb' moment. The first thing I thought was 'Man, I feel stupid. I should have been doing this years ago,' as we'd had a website up for over ten years, and I couldn't believe we hadn't been doing this. It's crazy because it's so simple. The connection of answering people's questions is such a simple concept. But executing it was something that we had just never done before."

So, it was in January 2013 that I met with much of Novak's company and introduced to the team the philosophy of They Ask, You Answer and the potential impact it could have on the company as a whole as well as the individuals, assuming everyone embraced this "teacher's mentality." Novak has since attributed that workshop as the pivotal moment when Segue Technologies' online efforts, and entire business model, began to shift.

After the workshop, Novak showed just how serious he was about this new philosophy by making it mandatory that every employee in the company contribute to the company's content strategy. Each employee was tasked with writing at least one blog per quarter for a total of four blog posts per year.

We wanted to get everyone involved. Whether they were going to be great writers, or whether they were going to be people who were going to do it long term, I just wanted to at least try it. Obviously we had some people that took to it and enjoyed it. We had some people who didn't enjoy it as much, and others who may have not loved it, but saw the value of it, especially once their articles started ranking and we started getting leads from their articles.

The Snowball Begins

Within a short time, Segue's newly focused content marketing efforts began to pay off in ways they had always hoped they would. And the early success they found inspired the team at Segue to continue to strengthen and develop their newfound obsession with educating their customers.

> We had some pretty quick growth. Before we started this process we had less than 1,000 visitors a month to our website, and within three months of the workshop we had over 30,000. We had several articles rank at number 1 on Google within a couple of months, so that really got people energized. For me it was just kind of a no-brainer from the beginning, but actually seeing it happen—watching the leads increase, and not just the number of leads, but the quality of leads as we improved our funnel and optimized our lead pages—was amazing. It's been really fun to see it all evolve.

Segue Technology's Astounding Growth

As Segue Technologies continued their content marketing efforts, they began to adjust their focus from simply getting articles out online to curating specific messages that they wanted to get across to their most ideal customers.

> We got to the point where we had to tweak our contact pages, because we were getting so many leads, and not all of them were the right fit for us. Just the shear quantity of traffic and leads was blown through the roof. All of that traffic allowed us to be a little more choosy too. For instance, one of the things we did was to change our contact form. Where it asks for them to give the size of their budget for their projects, we actually raised all of our values on them so that we could home in a little closer to our ideal customers. We added additional questions as well. What it did was reduce the number of leads, but the quality of the leads kept getting better and better.

Improving the System to Produce Content

After they had amassed a large number of articles, Segue changed the method of how content was produced. They then took things a step further and began to refine some of their older posts and e-books with higher quality in mind.

When we first started producing content, we had an intern who we had brought on specifically to help curate, organize, edit, and make sure the publishing schedule was staying on track. And she was amazing and has continued to do really great things for us, so we promoted her to content marketing manager. She's the one in charge for really keeping it going. It's important to have a person in that type of role. We became a little bit looser on the number of articles everybody had to write, because we had developed quite a bit of content over the past few years, so we started focusing on refining the message. We may not be producing as many blog articles per month as we used to, but we're much more thoughtful about what we're writing about, and we're doing a really good job of going back to older content and updating them, and updating the subsequent e-books as we have a whole e-book strategy around our different service areas. And because we started doing that, we've seen huge gains not only in traffic, but in the quality of leads, especially over the last six months.

Many businesses may think that targeting only specific types of leads could hurt their business by reducing traffic and overall lead generation, but Segue views their new efforts as exponentially valuable.

What's different about us is that we're not a business that brings in a ton of new clients each year, especially in the commercial space. If we bring on four or six new clients each year, that's actually a lot, because the size of our business deals are pretty large. *A typical deal for us is anywhere from a quarter million to a million dollars.*

When companies truly understand the power of great content and the philosophy of They Ask, You Answer, they don't just stop at using their content to attract visitors to their site, they continually repurpose their content at every step of the sales funnel. Whether it's through e-mails, phone calls, webinars, or trainings, companies like Segue recognize the value their content has in guiding potential clients through the buyer's journey.

One surprising area that we've been able to utilize content is during "proposal season," which occurs every July and August. During this season, the government, and the DOD in particular, have a lot of money they have to obligate and execute before the end of the government fiscal year, which is September 30. It tends to be a very busy time period, and when we're responding to requests for proposals, we'll use content created in our blogs to help us with proposals, because we've already thought about the questions and addressed the answers. Using content that we had already created previously as part of our proposals really helped us flesh them out and get them finished quicker.

Another factor that has helped Segue separate themselves from the rest of the pack in their industry is that they've never shied away from producing the types of articles that addressed questions their competitors weren't willing to answer, specifically, the Big 5 mentioned in chapter 9.

It may not seem very bold now, but back in 2013, one of the first articles I wrote was, "How Much Does It Cost to Build a Mobile App?" Within two weeks that article ranked number 1 on Google. Since then, others have written about it, but at the time, no one was willing to talk about it. We've also done a whole series of articles that sparked somewhat of a battle between our lead iOS developer for Apple and an Android developer for Google Apps with a number of articles that addressed the question, "Which is better?" Other content has sparked quite a bit of back-and-forth debates in our comments sections. The article "Waterfall vs Agile: Which Is the Right Development Methodology for Your Project?" got a lot of people from both sides sharing some very strong opinions.

And with all of this, Segue continues to build its brand as one of the premier educators and thought leaders in their field. Today, they continue to set themselves apart from their respective peers by staying at the forefront of their industry, all thanks to their commitment to this business philosophy. And the numbers produced from their efforts proves that they're going to continue leading the pack for quite some time.

When we first started doing inbound marketing and They Ask, You Answer, we were getting around 1,000 visits to the website each month. Last month we had 85,000. And when we started tracking all of the revenue that could directly be attributed from inbound marketing, *it came out to $8,053,442.31.* And that's just since 2013. So, I think that's a pretty cool inbound story.

Eight million in additional revenue?!
Yes, that is a cool story.
Well done, Ron Novak and Segue Technologies.

13

Content Subject 2

Problems: How to Turn Weaknesses into Strengths

Now that we've covered the first subject of the Big 5—or the five content subjects that move the needle in every industry, let's move to the second one: problems.

You may be thinking, *What do you mean by "problems," Marcus?*

Well, the simple answer is this: When people buy, they worry more about what might go wrong than what will go right. It's true. It is for this reason that, for example, when someone is buying a 2017 Ford Mustang, their main searches would be either "2017 Ford Mustang Reviews" or "2017 Ford Mustang Negative Reviews."

But, what they would *not* search is *"Positive* Reviews 2017 Ford Mustang."

Make sense? In fact, I'd venture to say as a consumer you've searched by this point in your life hundreds of "negative"-based phrases, but no positives.

As buyers, although we want to know the good, bad, and ugly, we are mostly concerned with the ugly.

The same was true for me as a pool guy. Let's imagine for a minute that you had met with me back when I was a pool guy, and you had gotten a quote for a fiberglass swimming pool. Let's say you liked me as well as my pools, and you decided you might just want to buy one. But just to keep me honest, though, you elected to get a quote from a second swimming pool company—a concrete pool company. Let's call this company Concrete Joe's Pools.

Once you meet with Concrete Joe and tell him you met with Marcus, the fiberglass swimming pool guy, what do you think he's going to say about my fiberglass pools?

Of course, Concrete Joe is going to make such statements as:

- "Fiberglass pools aren't wide enough . . . or long enough . . . or deep enough."
- "You can't customize them." Or, "They crack." Or, "They pop out of the ground."
- "You don't want a fiberglass pool! They are not even real pools. It's like having a bathtub in your yard!"

And finally, he'll likely say something like, "If you buy a fiberglass pool, you're going to have nothing but problems, problems, problems. Don't get that pool if you don't want those problems!"

You might think I'm exaggerating with this scenario, but it's true. I saw it hundreds of times during my years selling swimming pools.

And when it does happen, as the buyer, you now have a moral dilemma. You liked me and you liked my pools, but after talking with Concrete Joe, you're a little freaked out worrying about all their potential problems.

So the question is, *What do you do next?*

Sure, you may ask a friend, but what you're most likely going to do is go to Google and search something like, "fiberglass pools problems."

14 | Addressing the Elephant in the Room

Since my first days as a fiberglass pool guy, one of the questions I got for years was, "Marcus, be honest with me. What are the problems with a fiberglass swimming pool?"

And for years, just as I had done with the cost question, I danced around the answer. But once we embraced the philosophy of They Ask, You Answer, I said to myself, *Enough is enough,* which led to my business partner Jason writing what turned out to be an epic article on the website titled, "Top 5 Fiberglass Pool Problems and Solutions."

Now, you might think it would be insane for us to write an article with that title and, believe me, so did many people in our industry. But look at it this way: How many of our competitors were addressing that question on their websites? Of course, the answer is none.

Yet, how many consumers were wanting to know the answer to said question?

Pretty much all of them.

The reason for these clear efforts to ignore such a question comes down to a psychological issue that almost all businesses struggle with, and that's the concept of addressing the elephant in the room.

Herein lies one of the great dilemmas of the digital age: Consumers are not dumb; nor are they ignorant.

If the marketplace believes (rightfully or not) that a product, service, brand, or other factor has problems—they're very likely going to find out.

As a business, you have a choice:

- You can allow the consumer to discover your elephant(s) themselves and in turn lose trust in you.
- Or, the minute they walk in the front door (or the virtual front door), you can say, "Here's our elephant. Do you have a problem with it?"

When we wrote this article, we said:

You know what? Buying a fiberglass swimming pool might not be for you. It might not be wide enough, or long enough, or deep enough. You might not be able to customize it to the extent that you want. But, if you're looking for a low-maintenance pool that is going to last you a lifetime, and you like one of the shapes and sizes that we offer, well then a fiberglass pool might be the perfect choice for you.

15

How Talking about Our Problems Generated More Than $500,000 in Revenue

The reaction to the problems post on our website was very similar to the cost piece. In both cases, consumers expressed their gratitude and ultimately gave us their trust.

Just like before, if they could have responded with their voice, they might have said, "Finally, *somebody* was willing to address this question!"

What was the result of that post? Well, in simple terms, over the past six years more than 260,000 people have visited our website because their search criteria related to "problems" with fiberglass pools. And thanks to the fact that we can track each one of those visitors who eventually filled out a "Request a Quote" form we also know this one article has generated well over $500,000 in additional sales since the day it was published.

You may be wondering how talking about one's own problems (flaws, negative reviews, and such) could generate half a million dollars, but the answer is simple, really. People trusted us because we were willing not only to address, but to embrace, the elephant in the room. And that, in and of itself, is power.

In closing, I ask you this: How many times over the years have prospective customers questioned you about any of the potential problems or issues they may experience with your products or services, or your company?

If they have asked you these types of questions, I guarantee you that thousands of others have searched those same issues online. I can also promise you that they are getting their answers from somewhere. Wouldn't it be better if they were getting those answers from you?

Putting It Into Action

Turn Your Problems into Strengths

This activity, similar to the others we've done up to this point, will not work unless you're truly in tune with the way your prospects and customers think. Nor will it work if you're not completely honest with your answers herein.

To start, answer the following two (very related) questions:

1. What does the competition say is a negative about the thing we sell?
2. What do consumers and buyers see as the negatives of our products and services? (Is it that you're the most expensive? Is your product only a good fit for certain applications?)

Once you've completed this, ask yourself: *How can we address each of these honestly and transparently on our website and within our sales process so as to turn it into an advantage?* Assuming you approach this the right way, the answer to this question (and the actions you take) could lead to some pretty incredible results for your brand and business.

16

Case Study 2

An Equipment Financing Company Becomes a Digital David and Conquers the Industry Goliaths

Another tremendous success story of They Ask, You Answer—especially when addressing the "problems" of an industry—comes from Rob Misheloff of Smarter Finance USA.

In a couple of years, Misheloff has worked wonders to transform his one-man financial loan information company into an inbound lead- and sales-generating powerhouse, all the while becoming a digital David in a land of financial Goliaths and proving himself nimbler, faster, and more creative than his behemoth counterparts.

Approaching his website content with a unique blend of helpful information, bold transparency, and more than a dash of his own brand of humor, Misheloff has been successful not only in educating his clients and growing his business, but he's been having a good time doing it too.

And like many who share similar success stories in the world of great content, Misheloff just kind of stumbled into it.

About Smarter Finance USA

Misheloff got his start back in 2003 when he formed a small reverse-mortgage direct mail company that sent out mailers to elderly people who were "house rich, but cash poor."

He loved his job because he felt that he was really making a difference in people's lives by offering them a chance to access their home equity while deferring mortgage payments until after their death. With reverse mortgages, elderly clients "no longer had to make the tough decisions of choosing between food and medicine, even though they owned their house," says Misheloff. However in 2013, changes to the product Misheloff was selling made it less viable, and Misheloff was left scrambling to find a new business.

Because direct mailing had worked so well for him in the past, he believed that he just needed to find a new market in which he could easily create a niche for himself.

Through a former employee, he heard about the equipment financing industry. But when Misheloff started digging into the financing trade to learn more about the competitors already in the field, he found something quite disturbing.

> One of the things I loved about my direct mailing business was that it was in an industry where most of our customers were really good people and they wanted the best for their clients. There were very few charlatans. We found that in the equipment financing industry from listening to our customers that *they were just being lied to by brokers and lenders.* These other companies knew that guys driving trucks didn't really know finance, so they could just tell them anything.

Misheloff wanted to be in a business that truly helped people solve their problems, and he "wasn't going to be in a business to help others steal from small business owners."

With this desire at heart, in January 2014 Misheloff made the decision to start Smarter Finance USA. This new company would help people looking to finance equipment for small businesses by giving them as much information as they needed to make informed financial decisions.

However, Misheloff quickly realized that his old tactics of using direct mailing to solicit new leads just wasn't as effective as it had been in the reverse-mortgage world he had previously occupied. And so, like many start-up companies looking to stake their claims in a new trade, Misheloff took to the Web.

I got started at the end of January 2014 and realized I needed to get some leads. I first tried some spam e-mails—they didn't work so well. Then I turned to PPC (pay per click/Google AdWords), which were a little successful in generating leads, but not really worth the price I was paying per click. With this method, I was able to get people to a one-page landing page and try to work the leads from there, but it's really hard to quickly earn the trust of someone trying to get a loan, especially because these people know absolutely nothing about you or your business.

Smarter Finance USA Embraces They Ask, You Answer

The philosophies of They Ask, You Answer came to Misheloff completely by chance as he was up late one night and saw a link someone had posted of my e-book, *Inbound and Content Marketing Made Easy*. With his wife and daughter asleep, Misheloff figured a quick look at the book couldn't hurt anything.

I actually ended up reading the entire book that night. It was the first time in my life I had ever read a book and said "This is literally going to change my life." And I didn't even know why I had so much faith, but I did. I just knew this was for me.

Within days, Misheloff and I were on the phone discussing his goals and planning out a strategy that would, in many ways, make him the king-pin of his space.

The principles of content marketing and They Ask, You Answer really spoke to Misheloff because they epitomized what he had felt all along, and what he found to be missing among his peers in his industry: *he wanted to bring truth and honesty back into online financing information*—and he planned on doing it better than anybody had before.

Misheloff didn't want to simply find financial success. He is one of those rare types who genuinely wants to help people in difficult situations get the best care they can, so that they have a shot at building a successful small business of their own.

Smarter Finance USA Focuses on Educating Small Business Owners Searching for Equipment Loans Online

Among the first pieces of content that Misheloff ever wrote were those aimed at dispelling the dishonesty found in so many of his competitors' rate quotes and to carefully explain to readers how they could avoid getting scammed while searching for equipment loans.

He focused on articles that explained the pros and cons of leasing equipment, how people can easily spot a loan scam, and he wrote other articles that detailed the problems with the leasing industry in general. Here are a few examples:

- "A Review of Go Capital: Are They Legit?"
- "5 Ways to Get Out of a Merchant Cash Advance (and Other Toxic Business Loans)"
- "5 Lies Heavy Equipment Financing Companies Tell You"
- "5 Restaurant Equipment Leasing Swindles to Avoid"
- "Gym Equipment Leasing: True Costs of Fitness Equipment Financing"
- "An Honest Review of One of the Best Truck Factoring Companies"
- "Private Business Loans: 5 Secrets the Big Boys Hope You Never Learn"
- "Contractor Loans: "7 Ways to Finance Your Construction Business"
- "Small Business Term Loan vs. Merchant Cash Advance: Which Is Best?"
- "Daily Payment Loans for Your Business: Do They Ever Make Sense?"

It's such a dirty industry. It's unregulated, and so people will outright lie to customers. You can even find it on the front page of Google. Some of the biggest companies in the industry always start by saying, "Our rates are 5 percent." But almost none of the people shopping online for equipment financing are ever going to qualify for a 5 percent rate. For a small business owner shopping online for financing, those rates almost never exist.

With such focus on exposing truth versus scams, Misheloff gained more and more respect from consumers for his willingness to address the industry's elephants, and in that process, he gained a phenomenal amount of trust. In fact, it became quite common that people would reach out to Misheloff after reading his articles on scams and then send him the contracts they'd received from leasing companies to ask if the contract looked fair.

"I see some of these contracts and they're total garbage designed to steal from people," says Misheloff. "It's really disgusting that this happens in my industry."

Misheloff has made it his mission to set the record straight about equipment leasing online, and in just a little more than two years has produced hundreds of articles and videos detailing how people can get financed for a wide variety of equipment.

Whether he's writing about how to get financed for dump trucks, limousines, food trucks, welding equipment, arcade games, forklifts, chiropractic equipment, or any other equipment for which a small business may need to find financing, Misheloff works hard to make sure that his content is thorough, informative, transparent, and even humorous at times.

He also prides himself on the fact that while some content marketers claim to knock out entire articles every day, he can spend up to three days working on a single piece of content. But he does it with the assurance that it's going to "be the best stuff that's out there."

I take subjects that have very low keyword value (aren't necessarily searched by many people), and make these huge articles out of them. I have multiple infographics that I make myself, and I add videos, and all kinds of other crazy stuff, because I figure that each article I write is going to produce leads for years. I'm not writing the articles for just right now, because right now it's actually kind of easy to rank for a lot of these things in Google because my competitors are still doing it the way they've always done it. But I know in a few years these same competitors will start to figure out that they really need to be producing content and answering consumer questions themselves, but by the time they get with the times, it's going to be tough to knock me off the hill, regardless of how large they are as an organization.

Smarter Finance USA's Educational Content Pays Off in a Big Way

And the proof of Misheloff's efforts lies in the growth that he has experienced in both traffic and in leads. In just under two years, Misheloff's site has been doubling nearly every two to three months in traffic, starting with just a few hundred visits at the beginning to more than 25,000 visits in late

2015. And during this time he has amassed more than 2,600 new contacts who have taken the time to fill out a form on his website.

Misheloff himself was even stunned by the number of leads he was getting every month and shortly realized that he wouldn't be able to work every deal himself.

For the most part, I don't even work the leads anymore, I get over five hundred leads a month just from the website and another hundred or two in phone calls. I don't have my own team, so what I do is farm the leads out to a few different companies that I think are the best fit for the types of leads I'm getting.

When asked about specific ROI (return on investment) Misheloff stated:

January 2015 (about six months in) was when I saw my first dollar of revenue from all the work I was doing.

First quarter of 2015 I ended up closing six transactions totaling $220,000 in fundings, resulting in $11,846 revenue. Not a lot, but this was enough to validate that money *could* be made.

First quarter of 2016: thirty transactions, $2,045,000 in fundings, resulting in $144,112 in revenues. A good chunk of that revenue is shared with affiliates, but what I am taking home for the first quarter of 2016 is about $55,000 in profit.

Misheloff knows that if he hired more staff and rented out a legitimate workspace he could broker most the deals in-house and keep the lion's share of the profit. But Misheloff is more concerned about maintaining the lifestyle that he has come to know and love.

When you're not paying for the leads, you have to ask yourself: "Am I more interested in maximizing my profits, or my happiness?" And for me, the answer is, "I just want to do it the inbound way." I don't want to open an office, or have a large staff, or spend my day talking into a phone, or have to drive into work every day. I get to work from home in shorts and a T-shirt. I don't have any stress; I don't have anything to worry about.

And not only that, but Misheloff, unlike many businesses, has always seen his size as a major advantage when embracing the digital consumer. Instead of all the red tape that typically comes with working for larger organizations, if he wants to talk about something, he talks about it. If he wants to get something done, he does it.

> You hear people saying how tough it is to make it on the Internet, and that you have to be some megacorporation to be successful—it's all crap! Just obsess over your customer. Figure out what they're thinking, asking, and going through. Then have the guts to address it. This philosophy has made me who I am, and offered me an extraordinary lifestyle in the process.

An extraordinary lifestyle and an even more extraordinary example of what one person can do despite an incredibly competitive niche. All in a day's work for Rob Misheloff.

17 | Content Subject 3

Versus and Comparisons

The third major content subject of the Big 5 is that of "versus" and/or "comparisons."

As consumers, we're fascinated with comparisons. We love knowing the best, the worst, and everything in between. And having all the information in the world at our fingertips has made this thirst even more prominent.

Just consider for a moment the last major purchase you made. Were you looking only at one option or multiple? If you're like most buyers, before you made the purchasing decision you researched multiple options; ultimately making your decision after stacking them up against each other and then choosing the one that you felt was best for your needs.

But you're not alone. Hundreds of thousands of comparisons are searched online every single day.

When I was a pool guy, the story was no different. In fact, our biggest competition wasn't other fiberglass pool builders, but rather concrete or vinyl liner in-ground swimming pool companies. Because fiberglass was "the new kid on the block," other pool companies would continually criticize it, claiming it was flawed, inferior, cheap, "not a real pool," and so on.

In fact, over the years, one of the top questions I received from potential customers was, "Okay Marcus, be honest, why would I get a fiberglass pool over concrete?"

For a long time, like most pool builders, I didn't address this question on our company website. We simply talked about fiberglass, and that was it. In hindsight, this was really, really dumb.

I can't even imagine how many potential customers dismissed us because they had received wrong, or inaccurate, information from another source. Furthermore, I don't know how many hours I had wasted on the phone and in person with shoppers who clearly were not a good fit for fiberglass. But because they didn't know any better, their time—and my time—was wasted.

Once we embraced They Ask, You Answer as a company, it became obvious we needed to address this major question. But what really pushed us over the edge was the following e-mail we received from a reader of the website:

> As you're no doubt well aware, it's a desert wasteland when trying to find information on pools. . . . Sorting through the Internet for usable information is difficult in the extreme. Of the few forums I've found, most devolve into trolls arguing gunite (concrete) vs. fiberglass vs. vinyl liner— over and over and over and over. What would help a great deal is to find some kind of unbiased information that explains each pool in detail and then backs off—letting me (or the customer) make the final decision.

So finally, after receiving this e-mail and hearing the same question hundreds of times over the years, we produced an article on our website entitled, "Fiberglass Pools vs Vinyl Liner Pools vs Concrete Pools: An Honest Comparison."

Once again, we were the first in our space to address the question.

And why were we first?

Simple—companies were focused more on their own fears and inadequacies than on what consumers really wanted to know.

Fiberglass pool builders were literally using the following logic:

> Our biggest competition is concrete swimming pools. So as to deal with this problem, we're not even going to discuss concrete pools on our website. And if we don't discuss them on our website, no one will know they exist.

Yes, you did just read that correctly.

And yes, that was the logic of fiberglass pool builders for years (and still, for many, to this day).

But as you can surely imagine, this example in the swimming pool space is replicated and followed in just about every other industry in the world. It's what we all do—a classic case of ostrich marketing.

We think if we ignore the problem (or question) that it will go away, but it doesn't. And ignoring it only destroys trust.

Remember: *Consumer ignorance is no longer a viable sales and marketing strategy.*

If we're counting on the idea that a prospect or customer isn't going to find out about that other option, sale, discount, brand, technology, methodology, or other factor, then we're sorely mistaken.

Just because a consumer might start out as ignorant (not informed), eventually they will become an informed buyer. In fact, many will get to a place where they're even *more* informed than the vendor or sales person they're dealing with.

It's a reality of the digital age.

And because of this reality, we have to live and do business by a different standard. We must say to ourselves, *Let's assume our prospects and customers know every single other possible solution, possible vendor, and possible competitor out there.* If we conduct our business that way, and design all of our sales and marketing messaging to be aligned with this philosophy, the possibilities are literally endless.

The Results

So what was the result of honestly comparing all types of swimming pools?

Well, as you likely already guessed, searchers (consumers) and search engines alike absolutely loved the content.

As a company, we received dozens and dozens of compliments from swimming pool shoppers after we published the article, expressing just how thrilled they were to finally read an "unbiased" review of the different types of pools. And with more informed shoppers who were able to truly understand the differences between the types of pools, we received dramatically fewer phone calls and went on way fewer appointments of "bad-fit" prospects—those for whom a fiberglass pool was clearly not the best option.

Along with this success, the search engines once again rewarded our willingness to address supposedly "difficult" questions. Even to this day, our website is the first to show up in a Google Search Engine results page when you type in:

- Fiberglass vs. concrete pools
- Fiberglass vs. vinyl pools
- Vinyl vs. concrete pools
- Concrete compared to fiberglass pools
- Concrete compared to vinyl liner pools
- And on and on

That one article has generated hundreds of thousands of dollars since the day it was written. But it is just one of many comparison-based pieces of content we've produced over the years, all because we've been asked so many times, "So tell me the difference between. . . ."

Putting It Into Action

Write down every question you've ever received from a prospect or customer who was asking you to compare two or more things. This could include products, brands, methods, companies, and other subjects. It could also include your products and services or ones you don't even sell. The key, though, is that you consider the many comparison-based questions that potential buyers and customers are asking (and searching) in your industry right now. Once you've made this list, address these questions honestly and transparently throughout your digital marketing efforts—be it with blog posts, e-books, webinars, and so on.

18

The Critical Need for Unbiased Content

Whenever I've taught audiences about the need to address the comparison-based questions we continually hear from customers, someone will inevitably say something like "It's impossible for businesses to address that type of question well. They're biased, and consumers know it."

Let me simply say this statement is fundamentally false.

Consumers *do* want to know what your business believes about these types of questions; otherwise, they wouldn't ask you the question in the first place.

But the response you give them . . . now that's where you've got to overcome this incessant need to brag, exaggerate, and only focus on why your company (or product, service, and so on) is the greatest thing since sliced bread.

So how do you do it? How do you immediately gain the reader's (or viewer's) trust while overcoming this hurdle of sounding biased? Well, let's go back to the example of writing an article (or producing a video—they're very similar in a way) that compares fiberglass, concrete, and vinyl-liner pools. If you're going to write an article like this, the proper way to do it might sound something like this:

Each year customers come to us at River Pools and Spas and ask us, "What is the difference between a concrete and a fiberglass pool?" This is a very good question. We can certainly understand the need to know the difference, as it is a choice a pool buyer is going to have to live with as long as they're in their home. Here at River Pools and Spas, we only sell fiberglass pools, but the truth of the matter is, a fiberglass pool might not be the best fit for you. In fact, a concrete or vinyl-liner pool might be the better option. What this article is going to do is explain the pros and cons of each type of swimming pool in an honest and transparent manner. This way, by the end, you'll be able to identify which is the best fit for *you*.

Disarmament: The Quickest Way to Build Trust

The principle at work in the opening you just read is a principle we've used many times with our clients all over the world, and that is the principle of *disarmament,* which is arguably the least understood element of great communication and copy—online and offline.

To understand the principle of disarmament, imagine you are negotiating in a hostage situation. As a trained negotiator, the first thing you ask the gunman to do (in most cases) is to request that he put his weapon down.

We've all heard this phrase in movies before, but believe it or not, it has serious significance in the world of sales and marketing too.

The reason for this is simple: In a hostage situation, unless someone puts their weapons down, it's almost impossible to communicate with them, much less earn their trust.

But once they do put their weapon down, the process of negotiation (trust building) can begin.

Believe it or not, it's much the same with sales and marketing communication—in order to make progress and earn trust, especially when the buyer senses the business is biased, proper use of disarmament is a must.

For example, if I'm going to write an article comparing fiberglass and concrete swimming pools (as shown previously), I must first eliminate the elephant(s) in the room, and I would do this by:

1. Stating first that our company sells *only* fiberglass pools.
2. Admit immediately that fiberglass isn't necessarily the best choice for everyone.

3. State that concrete pools might, at times, be the better option.
4. Explain how the article (or video) takes an honest look at the pros and cons of each, allowing the reader to therefore decide the best choice for them.

When you come out of the gate and mention these things, the reader will immediately sense the honesty (and sheer uniqueness) within the company or brand, and therefore place more trust in what is being said.

You should always look for examples of what is good about the *other* choice or option when explaining things to your prospects and customers. If you're willing to give them both sides of the coin, they will look at you as the trustworthy voice. And they are going to think, *This person truly does have my best interests at heart.* That is the essence of disarmament.

Let me again stress, though, that disarmament goes well beyond the things you say on your company website. Essentially, it's the way we approach customer questions with our business, be it face to face, online, or other situations.

For example, let's examine an offline scenario. Imagine you're in a sales situation and you've just made your pitch to the prospect. You've spent a good bit of time explaining all of your company's features, benefits, deliverables, results, and so on. She's seen your proposal is at the point of making a decision. But before she gives you the "Yes" you seek, she leans back in her chair, folds her arms (the classic defensive position), and asks one more question:

"Okay, you've explained all this to me very well but I have one last question. Why should I choose *your* company?"

Ninety-nine percent of the time, most sales professionals who hear such a question would immediately go into why they (company, product, solution, and so on) are the best. But the truly elite communicators understand the defensive nature of this question, and know that this is exactly what the person who asked the question expects to hear.

But to disarm the situation, the best response to such a question is quite the opposite:

Well, to be completely frank with you, we may not be the best choice for you. We have been talking about your needs and your situation and describing what we can bring to the table to address those needs. You have also done this with other companies. You've seen their prices and you've seen ours. So, by now, you probably have a pretty good feel for things. So the question is, do you, based on what you've now heard, feel we are the best option for you?

The answer that comes next will be dramatically more telling than any further pitch would ever be for the prospect. As buyers and consumers, we don't want to be told what to do or what to buy. Rather, we want to think we've educated ourselves enough to arrive at an informed conclusion. The best sales teams and companies in the digital age understand and embrace this reality.

19

Content Subjects 4 and 5

Reviews and Best in Class

Before we dive into the powerful elements of this chapter, let me just mention here that what you're about to read is a very, very different way of approaching business and consumer education than what most people are used to. It's not taught in MBA programs and it's certainly not the norm.

But that, in and of itself, should make it a good thing. After all, the most successful business innovations of the digital age happen time and time again when an organization elects to take the road less traveled, ultimately clearing a new path and a new way of seeing "the way it should be done."

And with that, we'll now discuss the final two elements of the Big 5: *Reviews* and *Best in Class*.

As stated in the previous chapter, as consumers and buyers we love to compare. We love knowing whom everyone else loves, hates, and how they all stack up against each other.

We're also obsessed with reviews.

Whether it's a website like Yelp, Angie's List, or even a print publication like *Motor Trend* and its *Car of the Year* award, we are a society that cares about pecking orders.

After having embraced They Ask, You Answer in 2009, as a business owner I started to look at the types of content that were experiencing success in multiple industries and I came to an interesting conclusion:

There was no Yelp or Motor Trend Car of the Year *award for the fiberglass swimming pool industry.*

Notwithstanding, ours was very similar to that of the car industry. You have a handful of manufacturers that make shells of pools. They're like the Toyota, Ford, or Chevy of the fiberglass pool sector. They manufacture and distribute their shells to the hundreds and hundreds of pool installers all over the world. And most installers, like us at River Pools and Spas, carry one or two of these brands at a time—competing with the rest in the space (just as in the auto industry).

But during this time, I noticed that if a consumer wanted to know who the best manufacturers were, there was no authority there to tell him.

Also, if a consumer wanted to know the best models and shapes these manufacturers were building, again, there was nothing in the market that was designed to help.

It was during this time my mind again shifted back to the core principles of They Ask, You Answer and I thought, *Consumers want to see these types of ranking systems. And they certainly want to know the best swimming pool shapes and sizes for their needs. Therefore, if they want them, it's my job to give it to them.*

And that's exactly what we did.

In early 2011, I experimented with this type of content when I published an article entitled "The Best Fiberglass Pool Design Awards for 2011."

To come up with this piece, I spent hours getting to know the different manufacturers in our space. I looked at all of their pool designs, focusing my attention on the various shapes, sizes, and unique features.

Next, I divided all of these designs into different classes, such as "Best Kidney Pool," "Best Free-Form Pool," "Best Diving Pool," and so on.

Once this was done, I formulated the article, awarding the various manufacturers I truly felt were "best in class" of that particular shape.

Although this in and of itself may not sound that innovative, keep in mind that the very manufacturers I was giving out "best in class" awards to were the same ones I was selling against every day as an installer.

Without reading any further, can you guess how these manufacturers reacted when this article was posted online? Needless to say, they were very surprised, and the reactions were mixed.

Many of those who were included on the list contacted me, thanking me for the inclusion.

Others who were not included on the list called me and said, "Marcus, I see we are not on your list of the best pool shapes in class. Why don't you come out to our facility and see our fiberglass pools?"

I'm sure there were others who did not contact me at all, but the end result was the same for each—before the day this article was published, I wasn't anywhere on their radar. Frankly, they didn't know me from Adam—I was just some thirty-one-year-old kid who was part owner of a little swimming pool company in Virginia.

But once I published it in an open forum, and they saw people were paying attention, now they couldn't help but to take notice.

Even funnier, some of these manufacturers, upon receiving their awards, were announcing on the home pages of their websites that they had won a design award for best pool in class.

At the same time, this article was a hit with consumers. Finally, they were given something that would allow them to choose the right pool based on their individual wants and needs.

This article was so successful that we've produced more like it every year, all with resounding success, and all of which continued to build the River Pools and Spas brand, authority, and trust with consumers.

Today, if you go online and search anything related to fiberglass pool designs, one of these articles will likely be the first thing you see in search engine results.

Even better, these articles have built hundreds of inbound links coming from other websites over the years, many of which are coming from the manufacturers we compete against on a daily basis.

Putting It Into Action

Highlight Others and Build Your Referral Network

Contemplate ways to make reviews work for your company. Are there any "best of class" types of content you could produce in your industry? Remember, if you've ever been asked to compare two things, then the answers is very likely "Yes."

Also, consider all of the companies within your industry or a similar industry that could possibly be referral sources for your business. Find ways, assuming they're respectable organizations with good track records, to highlight who they are, what they sell, and why they're respected in the marketplace. The key here is that you see yourself as more than just a subject matter expert within your industry, but someone who sees outside of your small circle and therefore has an opinion, expertise, and knowledge of those subjects that matter most to the consumer.

20 | Using Reviews to Establish Yourself as an Expert

Now that we've discussed how to build your referral network and industry authority by writing review-based content, let's look at an even more unorthodox (and shocking to some) approach to building your brand and business—one that demonstrates the essence of They Ask, You Answer.

Have you ever had a prospect say to you, "We like you, and we expect we may do business with you, but in case we don't, is there anyone else you might be willing to recommend?"

If you've been in business long enough, you've likely heard this question before. You also likely know that when most companies receive such a question, the natural response is, "But there is no one quite like us!"

When such a statement is made, you and I both know that the person asking the question is going to think, *Oh, come on. Seriously?*

About four years ago, I spent about two hours in a sales appointment with a couple. When I was done giving them my proposal they said, "Marcus, we really like you a lot. We do. And we think we're going to use you. But hypothetically speaking, if we don't use you, who would you recommend that we use?"

Alas, the last thing you want to hear as a salesperson.

That night, I did not earn their business. But I did have a long drive home. And on that drive, I thought a lot about that question, as well as our rule of They Ask, You Answer. Upon reflection, I said to myself, *Well, if they asked the question, I guess I need to answer it.*

When I arrived home at midnight that evening, I immediately sat down at my kitchen table and wrote the article, "Who are the Best Pool Builders in Richmond, Virginia (Reviews/Ratings)" and posted it to our site. In it, I listed the five companies I believed were truly the best builders in Richmond.

Before I go on any further, let me ask you a question. Do you think I included myself (River Pools and Spas) in that list?

If you answered "No," you are correct. Now before you go on thinking I'm crazy, let's analyze why I wasn't on the list.

The first and obvious reason is that the moment I put myself on a best-of list of any kind, I lose all credibility. Any trust I might have built with the prospective customer is now gone. And as we've established many times throughout this book, everything comes down to trust. So, no, I did not put myself on that list.

Furthermore, consider this: If someone starts reading that article, where are they? That's right—they are already on my site. In other words, I don't need to prove to them that I'm awesome. They can see it for themselves. They can figure it out very quickly whether they like me or not. And in this case, let's assume that you went online right now and typed into Google "Best Pool Builders Richmond, Virginia" —which is a very common phrase for pool shoppers in that area who are looking for a swimming pool. Upon doing this, you'd immediately see this article (which is ranked first for the phrase in Google search engine results) and click to read more.

You then commence reading the following:

Each year at River Pools and Spas, we meet with well over a hundred households in the Richmond, Virginia, area with respect to their inground swimming pool installation. And because so many folks know our thoughts and feelings on all things related to pool construction from this website, they often ask us, "'Who are some of the other builders and competitors in the area?" Never one to shy away from being blatantly honest about the competition, I provide you with a list of some of the companies that have a solid inground swimming pool building history in the Richmond area.

Many companies use every page of their website to try to convince viewers how superior and awesome they are. In reality, no one wants to hear (from you) that you're awesome. Rather, what consumers want is to look at your works, judge them, and then make their own decisions on just how great a company really is.

Now, you tell me. If you were a swimming pool shopper and read those first two paragraphs, what would your impression of the company be? Do they sound believable? Honest? In fact, could you go so far as to assume they might just be experts?

If you're like most people, you answered affirmatively to all three questions. Without the company needing to state it, you now feel like they are experts and thought leaders—all because they've shown you they're willing to answer a question, honestly and transparently, that no one else in their space is.

This goes back to what we talked about with disarmament, and this is the essence of content marketing:

Honesty and transparency are self-evident, and when done with the right intentions, have a profound influence on the business, brand, and bottom line.

21

The Impact of Discussing the Competition

You may be asking what the final results of "Who Are the Best Pool Builders in Richmond, Virginia (Reviews/Ratings)" are.

To put it lightly, the results have been profound.

First of all, as mentioned before, if you search anything to do with "Best Pool Builders Richmond, Virginia," this is the first result you see in Google.

But the second result is where things get really, really interesting.

Let's assume you went online today and searched for "Reviews Pla-Mor Pools Richmond, Virginia." (*Note*: Pla-Mor is our biggest competitor in the Richmond area.) Once you enter such a search query, the first result you're going to see is, again, that article.

In fact, today, whenever anyone is researching reviews of our competitors, they usually land on one of these articles (as we've now produced many) on our website. All this while outranking such websites as the Better Business Bureau, Angie's List, and others that often own the conversation about reviews in multiple industries, especially in home improvement.

To put it all in perspective, allow me to share the following story of a lady who bought a swimming pool from us a few years ago. Upon discussing her decision to go with our company, she said:

Marcus, the most interesting thing happened. I was so close to signing a contract with Pla-Mor Pools for my swimming pool. But before I signed the contract, I decided to go online and research their company. While I was researching their company, I immediately stumbled across this article you guys had written and thought to myself, *My goodness, these guys are so honest, I should probably call them too!*

Of course, you know the end result. That lady bought a $50,000 swimming pool from us. And she bought it all because she had a common question and we were the ones that had been willing to answer it—honestly and transparently.

The year it was published, that one little article resulted in $150,000 in sales. And still today, if you go online and research the best swimming pool builders in Richmond Virginia, we will probably be one of the first companies you come across.

Now, you may be thinking to yourself, *Yeah, but Marcus, aren't you afraid you've now introduced them to the competition?* And if you're thinking this, let's be clear about something:

If someone wants to know who your competitors are, roughly, how long will it take them to figure it out?

Maybe five seconds . . . if they're slow!

The reality is this: Consumer ignorance is no longer a viable sales and marketing strategy.

It just isn't.

I knew at some point the buyer would learn about my competitors, just like I knew at some point they'd realize there are three types of inground pools (concrete, fiberglass, and vinyl). Plus, I could see how addressing these types of questions would give us a chance at doing business with folks who never would have found us otherwise—just as the lady who almost bought a Pla-Mor Pool had done. But because we had addressed the question, we were now able to enter the conversation with her and many, many others.

To this day, we are still getting rewarded for taking this bold approach to They Ask, You Answer with new business every single month.

And finally, if you're wondering how our competitors reacted to these articles, I can tell you that over the years, I've heard from many of them, and the response is almost always the same:

"Marcus, I don't know why you wrote that article, but thank you."

As for me, all I can do is chuckle, knowing the simplistic power and impact of They Ask, You Answer.

Putting It Into Action

Embrace Review-Based and Best-of Content

Brainstorm the top competitors and companies in your space, and then take the time to write an article about the best companies in your field. Remember to stick to facts and stay away from opinions when discussing the competition on your own website. But the key here is your willingness to have the conversation and become the trusted source of your industry in the process.

22

Case Study 3

*Small Retail Appliance
Store Dominates Online
and Makes Millions*

If you were asked which company you thought was the biggest online thought leader in the kitchen appliance space, you'd probably assume that it was one of the major manufacturers you've been seeing in kitchens for years; names like General Electric, Whirlpool, Kenmore, and Frigidaire might come to mind. Worth hundreds of millions of dollars each, these companies, at least in theory, should "own" the digital space.

However, you might be surprised to learn that not only is the go-to consumer information source in the appliance space not one of the leading manufacturers, it's not a manufacturer at all. Rather, the company that is making a killing by providing educational articles, videos, buyer's guides, and e-books that are answering people's questions about appliances is a regional retail store located in Boston, Massachusetts.

About Yale Appliance

Yale Appliance has been selling to and servicing the people of Boston with all of their home appliance and lighting purchases since 1923. From the Great Depression of the late 1920s and early 1930s, to the dot-com explosion of the mid-'90s, to the Great Recession of 2008, Yale Appliance has persevered through it all.

So how does a local appliance store maintain longevity over such a long period of time while many other businesses in their field have been forced to shutter their doors during periods of economic decline? The answer is simple: They turned to their customers and started paying close attention to the habits, problems, and needs of appliance consumers.

Steve Sheinkopf, CEO of Yale Appliance, is a perfect example of a business owner who caught on to content marketing at an early stage, when he went to a conference called In Planet back in 2004.

> In Planet was the single greatest conference I've ever been to. HubSpot's conferences are amazing, but this one was really foretelling of the future. They were saying things like, "While social media isn't quite there yet for businesses, it soon will be." I also learned that the first thing a company needs to do is manage their reputation online, and the second thing is to find a way to control the conversation somehow.

In 2007 Sheinkopf decided it was time to start taking control of online conversations about home appliances by starting a business blog for Yale Appliances. Sheinkopf had always distrusted the measurability of traditional advertising, and he saw an opportunity with content marketing for a greater return on his investment and the possibility to measure that return with concrete numbers.

For four years, Sheinkopf was pleased with the online results he was seeing: a growing social media presence as well as a steady (albeit slight) uptick in monthly traffic.

And as much as he personally despised traditional outbound advertising, there were times when he believed that he had no choice but to turn it.

> I've never been sold on advertising, even though we were doing some radio and television ads, and buying space in the *Boston Globe*. We were spending a lot of money. When the recession hit, I had read somewhere that refrigerators actually sold better during recessions like the Great Depression, so we advertised even more, but we didn't really get anything out of it.

The recession forced Sheinkopf to reevaluate his business goals and plans.

> When I was struggling during the recession, we had to ask ourselves the same two questions every other business has to: "how do I reduce expenses?" and "how do I add revenue?" And it usually boils down to the same answers: I need to sell more, and I need to cut more. And that's really hard to do. Anybody with compassion hates to cut people.

It was during these tough economic times that Sheinkopf decided to explore further why his inbound marketing strategy wasn't producing the results he was after, so he turned to the Web for answers.

A CEO Becomes the Head of Business Development

Sheinkopf was reading articles about HubSpot when he stumbled across the River Pools story and decided to reach out to me to see whether having a workshop with his employees could help turn around his company's inbound marketing efforts. But as Sheinkopf states, our first conversation didn't quite go as he had anticipated.

> My first talk with Marcus was brutal. I thought I was pretty good at business blogging, and I was just thinking that maybe I could improve a little bit. So I sent him a few articles for review and he kind of just beat me down. Marcus said to me, "I can see that you do the work, and that you take this seriously, but the truth of the matter is you're not doing it right. And we're not going to talk about what you're doing right, we're going to talk about what you're doing wrong, and how you can fix it. Can you handle that?" I almost hung up on him right then.

On a personal level, as the author of this book, and now a close friend of Steve's, this statement gave me quite a laugh. But the truth is, Steve's content strategy was way off. It was almost the antithesis of They Ask, You Answer. Instead of focusing on what consumers were asking, thinking, and searching for about kitchen appliances, he was writing about everything from the business's point of view (and not the consumer's) and was therefore experiencing no momentum from his efforts. (This, by the way, is extremely common for businesses all over the world when they embrace an inbound culture with content marketing. Although they are producing content, they are still doing it in a biased, sales-based manner versus one that is solely focused on teaching, helping, and solving another's problems.)

Fortunately, Steve ended up embracing my earnest criticism of Yale's content marketing efforts, and after a few further correspondences, he decided to have me come out to his company and teach content marketing in the style that had worked so well with our clients and River Pools: They Ask, You Answer.

After Yale Appliance's workshop in early 2011, Sheinkopf and his employees began tackling their content marketing strategy with a reju-venated passion and a new purpose that consisted of a clear direction and attainable goals.

Part of Sheinkopf's new content marketing plan was to reevaluate his company's overall goals. He realized that in order to achieve those goals he would have to put the customers first, produce content that was helpful, and aid clients in their purchasing decisions. Specifically, he focused on the Big 5 content and knew that if he was going to become something like a "Yelp for kitchen appliances," he was going to have to address the same types of subjects they did. In fact, here is a list of just some of the extremely popular articles Yale published since embracing this strategy, all of which have been viewed over 100,000 times each:

- "The 5 Best Counter Depth Refrigerators"
- "The Least Serviced/Most Reliable Appliance Brands 2015 (Reviews/Ratings)"
- "The Best Compact Laundry for 2015 (Reviews/Ratings/Prices)"
- "Quietest Dishwasher by Decibel Rating (Reviews/Prices)"
- "The 5 Best Affordable Luxury Appliance Brands (Reviews/Ratings)"
- "KitchenAid vs Bosch Dishwashers (Reviews/Ratings/Prices)"
- "Best Front-Load Washers for 2016 (Ratings/Reviews/Prices)"
- "The 5 Best Bosch Dishwashers (Ratings/Reviews/Prices)"
- "The Best Induction Cooktops for 2015 (Ratings/Reviews/Prices)"
- "Best 30-Inch Professional Gas Ranges (Reviews/Ratings/Prices)"

Sheinkopf didn't just stop with a smarter approach to the type of content he was producing: he also made content production a companywide policy, going so far as to add mandatory content production into the employee handbook.

> Some people are bad writers, I get that. But the other good part of getting everyone to blog is, theoretically if everyone is blogging and really trying, they'll learn to get better. If you spend a month researching a topic, you're going to know what you're talking about on that subject. And if you know what you're talking about, you should be able to explain it to others.

Even though Sheinkopf made it company policy that everyone in the organization had to help in producing content, whether researching and writing articles, helping draft new ideas, or participating in video shoots, Sheinkopf himself has written a majority of Yale Appliance's content, contributing more than 1,600 of his own articles.

> People would often question why the CEO of a company was working so hard on producing content when there were over 140 employees that could have been handling it. I actually started to feel bad about it. But then I was talking with Ann Handley [author of *Everybody Writes* and *Content Rules*] and she told me what I was doing was a good thing. She said, "You're in business development." And I thought "yeah, that's my real job. I'm in business development." Some of my articles have now been read 10 to 20 thousand times, and my top article has been read over 800,000 times. I couldn't advertise for that. That's why I do it, because I'm in business development.

With their retargeted marketing efforts, Yale Appliance's website traffic, leads, customers, and revenue began to grow at an incredible rate, doubling nearly every year from 2011 until the present, when their traffic averages more than 600,000 monthly visitors in 2016.

Yale Appliance Tackles the Tougher Questions

A big part of Yale's success is indebted to their steadfast commitment to writing articles that genuinely help consumers make the most well-informed purchasing decisions possible, even if it means ruffling a few major manufacturers' feathers along the way.

If you want to read an article that manufacturers really hate, read my article on "The 5 Most Serviced/Least Reliable Appliance Brands." I take people through the whole process of what it's like to buy something, and what the problems they may encounter are. We don't just sell appliances; we service appliances as well. And because we service appliances we have actual service data that we can pull from a database that tells us which brands, makes, and models end up needing the most services and repairs.

Think about that for a second.

How many business owners in the retail space would be willing to openly publish the good, the bad, and the ugly of the very brands and products they sell?

How many would admit when one had a very high service rate?

How many would be so bold as to be specific to the problems of that particular appliance?

The answer, of course, is almost none.

But that's also why almost no one has experienced the extreme success of Yale Appliance. Simply put, they care only about becoming the most trusted source in the world for consumers when it comes to appliances. That's it, and they let the rest of the chips fall as they may.

For example, though Steve's commitment to transparency and honesty is adored by his customers, his articles don't always sit well with the manufacturers. On more than one occasion Steve has been threatened with legal action for his earnest reviews.

I've had brands threaten to sue me over claims I've made in articles, but I don't mind, because what I'm saying is the truth, and I have the data to back up my claims. So when I've been threatened by brands, I say "Okay, well, I guess we'll have to give you all of our documentation, but we want the same from you. We want your records too." And as long as we're right, nobody wants to do that.

Even though Sheinkopf's articles may appear to be hard hitting to some of the major appliance brands, Sheinkopf sees his articles as a potential wake-up call to the manufacturers to improve their products.

I just report what I see. It's not up to me to make their products. They should take the advice of what's wrong with it and build it back up so it doesn't break. Threatening to sue me? It's the dumbest mentality. You shouldn't shoot the messenger for delivering the message that other people are saying too. You can't fault me for saying it. They should take the advice and make improvements to their product. I'm not going to trash them with imaginary stuff. That would be irresponsible. What I'm trying to sell is truth and honesty.

Yale Appliance's Success with Inbound Marketing

Publishing articles based on truth, honesty, and transparency about appliances has served Yale Appliance very well. Today, Yale Appliances doesn't spend any money at all on advertising, and focuses all of its marketing efforts into its website, blog, and learning center. And, says Sheinkopf, the results have been amazing.

> You want to talk ROI? What is my ROI? My investment is simple: It's my time, it's my team's time. You put our salaries together and it's still way under what we could have spent for advertising, and we still would have needed someone to maintain that anyways. Just by looking at a customer's e-mail address (that was attracted through our content marketing efforts) and connecting it to a purchase, we can say that it's at least *10 million dollars in sales a year*. And that's with *zero advertising*.

When others tell Sheinkopf that traditional advertising really does work, he has a few strong words on the subject.

> People have always quoted me as "anti-outbound," but I'm not that at all. If you're getting a return on your investment through radio, home-shows, television ads, then all the more power to you. Typically when people say advertising works I say, "How do you measure it?" and they say, "It's impossible to measure." Then how do you know it works? People don't want advertising. They want to contact you when *they're* ready to contact you. There's a difference between me telling you I'm great, and somebody reading something and saying, "Wow, that was great." If you, the customer, say it, there's a better shot at me earning your business.

If I was to advertise saying "Shop at Yale because we have a sale" by buying an audience of 500,000, how many people in that audience are actually in the market to buy something? And of those people, how many are actually listening and not changing the channel or fast-forwarding? You're paying 500 grand for twenty people . . . maybe. Where's the ROI on that? It's not measurable. Inbound, assuming you use the right tools, is measurable, and we're going to stick with what works, and what we can measure.

And boy has it worked for Sheinkopf. In early 2016, Steve opened a second retail location near Boston, and he did it without any additional advertising.

Simply by obsessing over customer questions, and being willing to answer them better than anyone else in their space, they've climbed to the top of their industry.

Once again, a Digital David beats Goliath.

23

The Competition

Now that we've discussed the power of the Big 5 in detail, the question, of course, is whether or not your company is willing to address this new way of thinking.

Sadly, despite the overwhelming evidence that has been shown herein, most people and organizations who read this book will not take such a transparent, consumer-centric approach to their sales and marketing efforts.

But the question is, *Why?*

Why won't more organizations follow this incredibly simple model of They Ask, You Answer when it's so very obvious buyers and consumers expect to have this information?

As I've consulted with businesses and brands around the world during the past five years, I've discovered there are three fundamental factors that dictate whether or not businesses are willing to be world-class listeners and teachers versus taking the opposite approach—a more traditional, closed-minded company-centric model—to growing their businesses.

I call these three factors "The Triangle of Influence":

1. The competition
2. The bad fits
3. The customer

Imagine an upside-down triangle that has three distinct sections, as shown in Figure 23.1. Each section represents a group that affects whether or not a company is willing to address a particular subject in their sales and marketing process—especially their online one. The top section is the

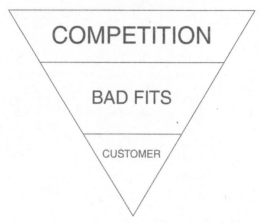

Figure 23.1   The Triangle of Influence

biggest and most influential factor influencing a company's reluctance to address the major areas of questions, problems, and needs of prospective customers. The middle section is less influential than the top section, and the bottom section is the least influential of all.

Based on what we've discussed so far in this book, who do you think is the main group of people (the top section of the triangle) that affects whether or not a company is willing to address the questions—especially the Big 5—of their prospects and customers?

Before we discuss these three sections of the triangle, I am going to let you, the reader, guess where I am going with this. What would you guess is the most influential group of people determining what you will and will not talk about online and off?

Well, if you guessed the competition, you are right. In other words, in chapter 10 when we talked about addressing cost and price on your website, you may have thought to yourself, *I can't possibly do that because the competition will see what's written and use it against me with buyers.*

Then in chapter 13 we discussed problems and issues with your products and services and the importance of talking about these problems. Again, you likely said to yourself, *If we openly talk about the pros and cons of our products and services, the competition will use it as a competitive advantage.*

In chapter 17 we talked about the importance of comparing products and services (like fiberglass and concrete swimming pools), as well as the need to admit when you're not the best fit for a prospect. Once again, you may be thinking, *I can't possibly introduce them to alternative solutions to my products and services that my competitors are selling.*

And finally, in chapter 19 we talked about addressing the competition directly, as we did with our "Who Are the Best Pool Builders in Richmond, Virginia (Reviews/Ratings)" article With this one, the most controversial and unorthodox of all you may have been thinking, *I can't possibly talk about my competition on my site! If I do, the prospect will learn about the competition and instead of choosing me, they will choose them.*

It is for these reasons that the competition is the most influential group affecting what most businesses will and will not address online today.

Think about that for a second.

The same group that has the greatest impact on a business's willingness to discuss what their prospects and customers want to know is the very group they're selling against, and the one that is already taking some of their business. In many ways, it's a case of double jeopardy.

People ask me all the time, "Marcus, if I start doing this—being honest and transparent and answering all these questions—what will happen if the competition sees what I'm doing and they do it, too?

Well, let me give you an example of how this works. Before I started my digital marketing agency and before I started speaking to so many groups and conferences, I was speaking to the swimming pool industry on this subject. So, believe it or not, everything that you have read in this book up to this point I have taught to pool companies all over the country in workshops at annual industry conferences. Even more interesting, many of the attendees of these workshops were the very companies I was competing with on a daily basis at River Pool and Spas in Virginia.

I once did the math and concluded that I had taught the principles you've been reading in this book to well over a thousand swimming pool companies.

Based on this fact, how many of these companies do you suppose followed the principles of They Ask, You Answer even half as well as we did at River Pools and Spas?

The answer: One or two . . . maybe.

This is an example of the saying that you can lead a horse to water but you cannot make it drink.

And that's the moral of the story. Well over 90 percent of the time, even though they've been taught or shown how to do it, businesses won't embrace They Ask, You Answer. It makes me sad to say it, but it's true. They have the knowledge, but they won't do it for themselves.

Why not? The reason is twofold:

1. They're thinking like business owners, not teachers. Teachers see the world differently. That's just a fact.
2. They come from a scarcity mentality and don't believe there's room on top for everybody.

In my case, I wasn't afraid my competitors would use the They Ask, You Answer principles; I was afraid they *wouldn't* use them.

So I taught the entire swimming pool industry. I wanted to help these companies despite the fact that they were competing for some of my very own customers. As far as I was concerned, truth is truth, and it wasn't mine to keep.

Furthermore, to me at least, it was just a matter of common sense. And in this case, common sense told me that giving people what they want, as honestly and transparently as possible, was the best way to do business, regardless of its *supposed* ramifications.

The Bad Fits

The second most influential group that dictates our communication and ability to teach as businesses online and off is more subtle. Oftentimes, we don't even realize that they have a major impact on things.

Let me give you a specific example of this influential group. If I say to you, "You should address the subject of pricing and costs on your site," a natural response, without knowing the benefits we've discussed would be, "Well, Marcus, if I address the subject of pricing and costs on my site, I will scare customers away."

Let's think about this statement.

"I will scare customers away."

But are they even customers at all? The answer, of course, is no.

Look at it like this: If your products and services start at $50,000, and that person has a true budget of $20,000, do you think he is magically going to come up with an extra $30,000 for your products and/or services?

In most cases, the answer is no. Instead of scaring the person, you're going to educate him, which brings relief and saves time for all parties involved.

What we are talking about here is being honest enough to allow—that's right, *allow*—the prospective customer to discover on their own that they are a bad fit for *you.*

If you've been in business any length of time, you know as well as I do that not everybody is a good fit for you. In fact, the most successful companies have a very clear understanding of the fact they aren't a good fit for everyone and therefore embrace this reality instead of resisting it.

The moment a business thinks it wants to do business with everyone is the moment that business starts to become very, very unhappy. Conversely, one of the happiest moments in the life of any business is the moment that business realizes what it is *not,* and who is *not* a good fit for it, and then lives by that awareness.

In fact, if you think about all the "bad customers" you've had during this time who were not good fits for you, there's a very good chance that you realized, before they ever became customers, you were receiving impressions in your gut that told you, *This person or company is not a good fit for us.*

Notwithstanding that impression, you still did business with them. And the reason for this was that you needed the cash flow at the time.

Then, when things between you and the customer deteriorated and stress mounted, and you stopped enjoying working with them, you got out of bed grumpy and said to yourself, *The money isn't worth it!*

This is why, even though it's important for a business to know what they are, the happiest businesses in the world have a deep understanding of what they are *not.*

That's right: the second most influential group that dictates what we do and don't talk about is made up of the bad fits. We allow those people, *who will never become our customers,* to dictate our ability to listen, communicate, teach, and help. And it's a tragedy.

The Customer

The only group that we *should* allow to dictate what we as businesses do and do not communicate to our customers (both online and off) is also the *least* influential group: the actual customer.

Yes, the person who is giving us their trust, money, and even referrals is the one we often overlook and ignore.

As you look at the triangle in Figure 23.1, tell me, what's wrong with the diagram? The natural reaction would be to say, "Marcus, it should be flipped the other way around."

When I first started teaching these principles, that's what I thought as well. Then I realized I was completely wrong. There should only be one group inside the triangle: the actual customer, as represented in Figure 23.2

When all is said and done, they are the only ones who truly matter.

They are the ones who will keep your lights on.

They are the ones who will allow you to live in financial peace.

And no one else.

Until the day your competition is paying your mortgage, and those bad fits who will never become your customers are funding your payroll, I urge you to consider focusing on the only group that truly matters.

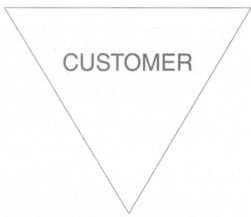

Figure 23.2   The Actual Customer

24

How They Ask, You Answer Saved River Pools and Spas

At this point, you may be wondering what the final impact of They Ask, You Answer was on River Pools and Spas.

As mentioned at the beginning of the book, in March 2009 we at River Pools and Spas were getting ready to lose our business. After learning about inbound and content marketing, we embraced what we called "They Ask, You Answer," and brainstormed every single question we had ever been asked by a prospect or customer. Night after night, after having heard multiple questions during the day from prospects, I (along with the help of my business partners) would write articles and produce videos addressing these questions.

When we first started this process, we were getting about two thousand visitors a month, and most of that traffic was coming from pay-per-click traffic on Google. We were spending about $500 every two days, and the money had finally run out.

But within three months of beginning to generate content, our site's organic (free) traffic began to double. Then, month after month, it just kept getting better.

Although 2009 was our toughest financial year as a company, we managed to survive. Our focus on content and great teaching was just enough to scratch and claw our way to at least keeping the lights on.

By 2010, I could see the work was starting to pay off. Our traffic and leads had exploded. The sales began to pour in.

Fast forward to today:

Today, River Pools and Spas has thousands and thousands of inbound links coming from other sites—even though we never attempted a "link-building" campaign to increase these numbers. This all happened simply because other sites and companies thought our content was useful and helpful enough to link to.

In 2014, our traffic peaked in the month of July with 350,000 visitors to our site.

In July 2015, it reached more than 500,000 visitors.

And in 2016, we crossed the 600,000 visitor threshold.

Today, River Pools and Spas is the most trafficked swimming pool website *in the world*.

Not only that, but in 2015, because of the tremendous growth, it was a natural progression for us to begin the manufacturing process as well.

Now, instead of just being a small installer of fiberglass swimming pools, we are in the process of developing a base of dealers throughout the United States. Based on where we are today, my guess is that, within the next five to seven years, we will become the largest manufacturer of fiberglass swimming pools in the world.

In conjunction with this, I share a couple of other statistics about River Pools and Spas that may astound you. In 2007, when home values were inflated and anybody could get credit to buy a swimming pool, we did about $4 million in business. In order to do $4 million in business, we had to spend about $250,000 on our advertising and marketing efforts.

In contrast, if you fast-forward to 2014—a time when most swimming pool builders were still dramatically down from the pre-recession time period—we did about $5.5 million in business, and spent roughly $20,000 on advertising and marketing.

So, when people ask me, "Marcus, what will be our return on investment if we follow the principles of They Ask, You Answer?," I can only laugh. I am someone who has been there and done everything I'm sharing with you. And, everything you have read up to this point in the book saved our company and helped make it what it is today.

Today, when I look back at the crash of 2008, I do it with an incredible sense of gratitude. Those low moments forced me to look outside of myself and the industry, and forced us, as a company, to do things as they had never before been done in the swimming pool space.

What is crazy about all of this is that we are just a small swimming pool installation company in Virginia with about thirty employees, and yet we're dictating the education of swimming pool shoppers all over the world.

Every day at River Pools and Spas, we receive e-mails from people all over the globe who want us to install their swimming pools.

Even though I am no longer in the swimming pool industry full time, I still receive these e-mails from places as far removed from Virginia as Australia, Europe, and the Virgin Islands. These e-mails often say something along these lines: "Marcus, we just don't trust our swimming pool contractor. Would you come out and oversee our swimming pool installation?"

Long before I became Marcus the Sales and Marketing Guy, I was turning down these requests, even though people were willing to pay me lots of money just to go out and oversee their swimming pool installation.

Why would I say no if I was being offered so much money to simply be an overseer? Well, I'll let you in on a little secret: *I can't install a pool.* I can't even turn on our excavator at River Pools and Spas. I am probably the worst pool builder in the world, and believe me, I'm the last person you want to see installing a swimming pool in your backyard.

But what I can do is look at how things are done with our installers (the real experts), ask them about what they're doing, and explain it in a way so that the average person understands how it is done. Because I am able to distill the facts into simple-to-understand words that pool shoppers find helpful, they naturally think I am one of the foremost authorities in the world.

Someone once told me, "It's dumb not to dumb it down."

At the time, I had no idea how right they were.

Since that moment, I've seen again and again how, when it comes to great marketing and communication, the moment a business or brand tries to sound smart is generally the moment they start to look stupid.

But when you don't try to sound smart, and instead look to have communion with your listener, that's when the magic happens. For me, this is my singular goal and obsession as a professional speaker, marketer, and communicator.

My point to you is this: Think like a teacher. Obsess not just over their questions, but the way you answer them. It will make all the difference.

PART

II

The Impact of They Ask, You Answer on Sales Teams

Up to this point in the book, much of what we have discussed has to do with the marketing side of They Ask, You Answer. But when all is said and done, getting found on Google and increasing traffic, leads, and trust is just one of the many benefits of creating a company culture of obsessive listening and teaching.

In fact, the biggest benefit to this type of business philosophy has much more to do with selling than anything else.

But this only makes sense. When all is said and done, regardless of the increased traffic and leads great content produces, if you're not generating new business, the end result is a failure.

As businesses, we *must* generate a profit. Having personally looked over the cliff called "Bankruptcy," I can attest to the truthfulness of this statement.

In this part of the book, we analyze how the principles found in They Ask, You Answer go well beyond your marketing department, permeating your entire sales team and organization when done properly. We show you its impact on sales teams, their culture, their ability to close, and exactly how you can better use content to dramatically increase your sales numbers.

111

25 | How Great Content Is a Total Game-Changer for Sales Teams

Let's assume for a minute that you're committed to making content marketing and the principles of They Ask, You Answer work within your organization.

In order to make this happen, not only do the leadership and marketing teams have to be aligned in their vision, but the sales team must immediately get involved in the process.

In order to do this, they must understand the what, how, and why of this important business strategy. Additionally, they must realize that there are multiple reasons why embracing this way of selling will affect not just the organization, but each sales person individually as well.

Listed next are seven benefits that sales teams need to understand will occur if they're properly integrating They Ask, You Answer into the sales process.

Seven Major Benefits of Sales Teams Embracing They Ask, You Answer

1. Producing Content Forces Us to Understand the Buyers and the Way They Think

If you're going to be good at content marketing as an organization, you better be *great* at understanding exactly what prospects and customers are saying, thinking, feeling, and searching. You must know their pains, worries, issues, and desires. Simply put, you must be dialed in.

In the marketing space, one might call this "buyer persona." But regardless of what it's called, many organizations and sales teams never quite reach a point where they are completely in tune with the way their customers and prospects think before, during, and after the buying process.

But when companies are forced to think about these things while they're attempting to produce educational and helpful content aligned to each phase of the buyer's journey, the ability of the sales team to put themselves in the shoes of their prospects and customers will never be higher.

In sales, empathy is everything. When someone doesn't have it, they generally aren't very successful. And when they don't have it with their content, it generally doesn't work either.

2. Producing Content Is Magical Practice for Sales Messaging

The best sales professionals have not only heard most questions a prospect could ask, they tend to answer them the same way each time. Furthermore, their answers are clearly stated and communicated in such a way that the prospect understands what was said, and their concern has now been resolved.

This type of effective communication is needed for every great sales pro, but it doesn't happen immediately, and it certainly takes practice. It is for this reason that content marketing can be so powerful: It helps the sales pro (as they produce the content) learn how to better answer the question, explain it in an intelligible way, and get the desired results they're looking for.

Here at the Sales Lion, we've heard time and time again how our clients improved overall sales communication *after* their sales team became involved in the content production process.

3. Company Content Acts as the Guide for All Training, Messaging, and So On

Even though sales departments have always been considered the financial heartbeat of most organizations, and even though their ability to have uniformity in what they communicate and teach to clients has always been extremely important, most companies have never taken the time to write out their "sales doctrine" for all their employees and sales pros.

As you might imagine, this is where content marketing and They Ask, You Answer come into play. Through in-house articles, videos, and so on, current and future employees have a database of training content that will help them to learn the company doctrines and philosophies faster and more effectively, affecting the human resources side of the organization for years to come.

4. Assignment Selling

It's a crying shame just how silo-driven many organizations are. Marketing sticks with marketing, and sales sticks with sales. But the fact is, the most successful companies understand that not only should the two be aligned, but sales should be using the content produced by marketing in their entire sales process. The concept of using content intentionally to educate the consumer and push them further down (or out of) the sales funnel is what we at the Sales Lion call "assignment selling." We discuss assignment selling in more detail later in this section.

5. Sales Teams Can Learn What Prospects and Customers Truly Care about . . . Before They Even Enter the Sales Funnel

With the plethora of advanced analytics and other tools that are available to sales teams today, there is absolutely no reason not to take advantage of deeper lead intelligence. For example, assuming a lead has filled out a contact form on your website, advanced analytics allow you to see every page that person has viewed on the site. It allows you to know how many times they've visited. It can also notify you every time they return to the company website in the future.

By looking at these analytics, a sales pro can start to piece together the "story" of the prospect long before the initial contact or phone conversation. This reality can be an absolute game-changer for a sales team.

6. With Content, the Relationship of Trust Can Be Built with the Sales Person (and Company) Long Before the First Sales Meeting

Every sales pro wants better leads. They also want to go on better sales calls. Unfortunately, many sales calls and presentations are focused—at least for the first part of the meeting—on building relationships of trust (instead of the "selling" part). But with the digital consumer of today, it's possible to build that trust (much more, in fact, than in a twenty-minute conversation) long before the initial sales meeting. This allows a sales pro to do what they do best: sell.

7. Great Content Means More Trust, More Trust Means Shorter Sales Cycles, Shorter Sales Cycles Equals Happier Sales Teams

Not only does every sales pro want more (good) leads, but they also want more *time*. Time to spend on more qualified opportunities. Time to spend with their families and loved ones. Time to do the things they enjoy most.

Fact is, great teaching (content marketing) can be the ultimate "time giver" to a sales department.

In the following chapters, you'll see some astounding examples of how using content in the sales process can not only save time, but it can have a tremendous impact on sales cycles and closing rates in general.

This is the essence to understanding just how much impact content marketing can have on a sales team and organization. And once companies start to understand these definitive benefits while engaging their sales team in the content production process, magic will assuredly happen.

26 | A Dramatic Discovery

Let me start by asking you a very important question:

On average, how many pages of your website do you think someone would be willing to read before they do business with you?

This is a question I've asked audiences all over the world. And in every industry and every country, I get pretty much the same answer: "Two or three pages."

Let's look at that figure. How long do you suppose it would take someone to read two or three pages of your site?

Conservatively, let's assume the length is about five minutes.

What you're really saying when you say that you can only envision a prospective customer reading (on average) two or three pages of your site is this: "Marcus, doing business with us is worth about five minutes of someone's time."

But do you really think the process of deciding to do business with you is worth *only* five minutes of someone's time? I'd certainly hope this isn't the case.

Fact is, as businesses, we grossly *underestimate* people's willingness to consider information in their quest to become informed and comfortable with a buying decision. To help you understand this point further, let me tell you about a dramatic discovery I made in 2012 related to my swimming pool company—one that has since affected many, many other businesses with its universal effectiveness.

At the beginning of 2012, I was comparing two groups of people who had filled out the "I want to get a quote" form on my swimming pool website.

By doing this, both groups of people had shown they'd gained enough trust to potentially want to do business with us. But here was the difference between the two:

- The first group filled out a form but ended up *not* buying from us.
- The second group filled out a form and *did* end up buying from us.

As I was looking at these two groups of people, I kept asking myself again and again:

What was the differentiator? What makes some buy but others not? What was the key indicator that would lead someone to say "Yes"?

As I was using HubSpot (more about them later) to look at the analytics on our site, I discovered something interesting about the number thirty related to the second group—the one that had bought swimming pools from us.

Can you guess what the number thirty represented?

If you guessed, "total pages viewed," you hit the nail on the head.

Now you may be thinking, "Wow, thirty pages is a lot!" That's certainly what I though when I discovered this anomaly.

Specifically, here is where it got interesting:

We discovered that if someone read thirty or more pages of the website before the initial sales appointment, *they would buy from us 80 percent of the time.*

By contrast, if they didn't read thirty or more pages, the average closing rate in terms of appointment-to-sale was only 20 *percent*

This was a phenomenal discovery. For me, in that moment, my entire relationship with this thing we call "content" reached a much deeper understanding and appreciation. It also made me rethink our entire sales process.

Such a stat begs the following questions:

What is happening over the course of a prospect reading thirty pages that caused such a dramatic increase in terms of their closing rates? And why is there such a big difference between the prospects who didn't read thirty pages of our site and those who did?

You have to look at it like this:

- Every time someone consumes a piece of your content (video, article, podcast, and so on), the trust factor continues to rise. Throughout that entire process, they are essentially "self-qualifying."

- Every piece of content that someone reads or watches becomes the equivalent of another meeting—or "date" —with that person.
- If you go on enough dates with someone, eventually, you'll get "married."
- Or you will break up.
- One way or another, over the course of thirty dates, you're going to clearly discover whether or not you're a good fit, and whether you want to continue forward with each other. The same thing is true with great content.

That being said, let's say that you found out that all you had to do was get a prospect to consume thirty pieces of your content (articles, videos, and so on) and they would buy from you 80 percent of the time. If that were true, what would you do differently? How would you handle that information? And how would that change your sales numbers?

The answer to these questions is what comes next: *assignment selling*.

27 | Assignment Selling

Often, when businesses embrace content marketing and They Ask, You Answer, the tendency is to think, *Okay, I'm just going to post this on my site and great things are going to happen!*

Unfortunately, publishing content on your site simply is not enough. You can't just passively post content on your website or social media channels and expect it to work its magic. You must find ways to actively help your prospects and customers read and view your content if you're going to truly move the needle. Furthermore, you cannot be passive about this, and you can't just leave it up to chance.

The process of actively using your content in the sales process is what I've dubbed "assignment selling."

To help you catch the vision that is assignment selling, we'll again use swimming pools as an example. But before we go any further, let me explain what I'm talking about when I use the phrase "assignment selling."

I define assignment selling as the process of intentionally using information:

- That you have created via text, video, or audio
- That is educational about your products and/or services
- With the purpose of resolving the major concerns and question of the prospect so they are dramatically more prepared for a sales appointment (or multiple sales appointments)

I reference this as something to do before and during the sales process.

An Example of Assignment Selling in Action

As you read the following, I don't want you to think you necessarily have to apply this to your business *in the exact same way* that I show here. The key here is the principle that relates to the way information or content is used to help your prospects either move down the sales funnel and advance, or become disqualified because they discover they're not a good fit for you.

Here is how it works: It used to be that someone would call my swimming pool company and say something like, "Hey, Marcus, I'm checking out your site and I think I'd like to get a quote for a swimming pool. Can you come out to my house this Friday and give me a quote?"

After asking them a couple of qualifying questions, I would say, "Sure, I'll be right out." I did that because that's what I thought sales people were supposed to do. If I was asked to go out and sell, I wanted to immediately go out and sell. Simply put, I didn't know any better.

This occurred because I wasn't truly thinking about the readiness of the prospect. I wasn't asking myself, *Well, wait a minute here. How much does this person really understand about the world of swimming pools?*

When I responded immediately to their request for a swimming pool quote, I had no way of knowing how educated they were with respect to buying a swimming pool. A person might be very informed and educated regarding our products and services, or they might be totally ignorant and aloof. I really knew nothing about my prospects and customers, and for all I knew, they knew absolutely nothing about that thing I was trying to sell them.

But I was not alone in my struggles. Many sales professionals are experiencing this very thing to some degree or another.

So, how does one overcome this? How does a sales professional take a prospect from "uninformed" to "*extremely* educated?"

At River Pools, we changed our entire sales conversations, starting with the first call. This is how it now sounded:

POOL SHOPPER: Hey Marcus, I've been checking out your site and I think I'd like to get a quote for a swimming pool. Can you come out to my house this Friday and give me a quote?

ME: Of course, I would love to come out to your house this Friday and give you a quote. However, you're getting ready to spend a lot of money on a swimming pool, and I know you don't want to make any mistakes with a project of this magnitude. So as to ensure you don't make any mistakes, we're going to help you become well educated.

In order to do this, I'm going to send you an e-mail. In this e-mail, you're going to see two main things. First, you're going to see a video of a fiberglass swimming pool installation. This will let you know how the swimming pool is going to show up to your house; it will show you the excavation and shell going in the ground; and it will also allow you to see the final grade-work and cleanup. In other words, you'll observe the whole process so that, when I come out to your house, you won't have to ask me, "So, Marcus, what does this process look like?" You will already know. That will save us both a lot of time.

The second thing I'm going to do is attach an e-book to this e-mail; it's essentially a buying guide. You will find this literature extremely helpful as well, as it will answer many of the questions you have right now. For example, it will address questions about what would be the best cover for your swimming pool: solid, mesh, or maybe even an automatic cover. The guide will also go over subjects like pool heaters and address questions of whether gas or electric is better, or whether you even need a heater at all. It's a little bit long—*about thirty pages*—but I promise you, it will be well worth your time.

Then I close by saying, "So, Mr./Mrs. Jones, would you take the time to review this e-book *before* our appointment on Friday?"

Having had this exact conversation with hundreds of swimming pool shoppers, I can tell you that 90 percent of the time, the simple response is "Sure."

At this point in the conversation, I would respond by saying, "That's great. Friday morning I will give you a call just to confirm our appointment as well as make sure you took the time to do those two things."

The Special Rights of the Teacher

You may think, upon reading such a statement, that asking a person to do this type of "homework" beforehand, and then letting them know you'll confirm whether they did said homework or not, is audacious.

I understand why you would say that. It is bold. It is audacious.

But it's also incredibly effective.

And the reason we have such an approach to selling is because our focus on teaching gives us the right to make such commitments with prospects.

First of all, in this case, I have taken the time to give this prospect tremendous value by producing a video that is going to walk them through the process of buying a fiberglass swimming pool. Second, we've created a guide that is going to answer the majority of their other pool-related questions.

There is an extreme amount of value in producing this content for them. And because I've done this, I've earned the right to ask more of the prospect, which, in this case, is to review the video and e-book.

But I couldn't, for example, say, "I found a book all about buying fiberglass swimming pools written by a guy in California, and I want you to read it before we meet."

First, the book I would be asking the prospect to read would not be filled with my words, and I would not have therefore earned the right— nor authority—to ask the prospect to read the book (or do the homework).

Second, by producing content in the form of text or video and posting that content on your site and other platforms, you take on the role of teacher. And the moment your prospects see you more as a teacher versus a salesperson, the amount of respect given dramatically escalates.

Remember: The rights of a teacher are greater than those of the person who does not teach.

You may be asking yourself, *What happens if they say, "You know, Marcus, it's great that you put together this e-book, but I won't have time to read it before Friday. Just come on out and give me a quote."*

How do you respond to that? Before you read the response, keep in mind here what I stated at the beginning of this section: *The way we are able to sell at River Pools and Spas may be different than the way you sell.* At River Pools, we can be a little pickier with our clients. Because we get a massive number of leads every day, we can qualify harder than other companies based on what we sell, who we sell to, and how much we have to sell in order to be successful.

That being said, we should all be looking for ways to help our prospects become more educated before we talk with them the first time, and then we continue to educate them throughout the sales process.

Here is our response at River Pools when someone says they don't "have enough time":

> Mr./Mrs. Jones, I appreciate the fact that you don't have the time to review this content, but here's the thing: Over the years, we have found that when our customers are very informed and take the time to review these things I am sending over to you, we have a wonderful experience when we meet with them in their homes. In other words, it makes for a much more productive meeting, and seriously eliminates buying mistakes on their part. This way, the customer is happy, and we are happy. But when they don't do these things, the experience is not nearly as good nor productive. So, Mr./Mrs. Jones, if you don't have time to become informed and educated about these things, then we are probably not the best fit for you.

As you read this, you may be thinking, *Really Marcus, do you actually tell them they're probably not the best fit for you?*

Yes, we do. And I can tell you exactly how they're going to react because I've heard such a response many times. In fact, everything you're reading about assignment selling and using content as a sales tool has been vetted and experimented with hundreds of times at River Pools and Spas.

Not only that, but this is exactly how we do things at the Sales Lion with our clients, giving us the opportunity to apply these exact same principles to large and small businesses and brands all over the world.

Remember, the principle of making sure we are dealing with educated prospects and customers essentially does not change from business to business, regardless of what you sell.

Now back to Mr./Mrs. Jones's reaction upon me telling them that if they don't want to become a bit more educated, then they're probably not the best fit for my business. I can tell you almost all prospects have responded in one of two ways:

- Response #1 sounds like this: "Okay, Marcus, fine. I will read your e-book and watch your video." And at that point I would say, "Well, that's wonderful! Friday morning, I will call you just to confirm you've done those things."
- Response #2 sounds like this: "Forget you! I don't need you to come out to my house and I don't need you to sell me a swimming pool. I'll go somewhere else!"

When this happens, your response as a business should be one of gratitude, because you now know they're clearly not a good fit.

Here is the core principle we are really discussing:

If becoming educated with respect to your products and services is not a variable in a prospect's buying decision, it almost always means they are basing their decision on what to buy solely on price. So unless your business model is one of being the lowest-priced guy every time, *the prospect is very likely not a good fit for you.*

What Homework Can Tell Us about the Prospect

By this point, you may be thinking, *But, Marcus, what happens if you call the prospect on Friday morning to ask if they did their homework and they say, "Well, no, I haven't done it, but I still want you to come out and give me a quote." What do you do then?*

That's a very good question, and that situation has happened many times as well.

When I first started this process, and a prospect would tell me, "I am so sorry, I got busy. But I still want you to come out and give me a quote," the salesman in me would think, *Well, they didn't take the time to do it, but I guess I can still go out there.*

I tracked those sales appointments over the course of six months, and I was shocked at the results. Guess how many of the prospects who failed to do their homework but said "Come out anyway and give me a quote" turned into customers?

If you guessed fewer than 5 percent, you are correct. This goes back to my point:

- Homework (education) can tell us a lot about the prospect.
- When people don't take the time to become well educated, they are most likely making their decision based solely on price, which generally means they're not the best fit.
- When it comes to success in business, the difference between happiness and frustration comes down to knowing who is, and who is not, a good fit for your organization.

28

How One Remarkable Couple Changed My Perspective on the Power of Content to Sell

Now that we've established *how* to do assignment selling, let's revisit one of the first questions we asked in this section:

On average, how many pages of your website would a potential client or customer be willing to read?

Well, the following story is an example of what is possible. It's also, in many ways, going to sound unbelievable, but trust me when I say it's absolutely true.

I'm giving you an example of a customer experience I had that really changed my perspective in terms of the way teaching can affect the sales process, as well as the willingness of shoppers to consume information in order to become comfortable with a buying decision.

About five years ago, when I was still a pool guy, I was up late one night using HubSpot to look over the leads that had come in to my swimming pool website that day, and one of the leads was from a man named "Mr. G." I saw that he had come to the site because he was searching on Yahoo for the phrase "cost of a fiberglass swimming pool."

But once he got to the website, something very interesting happened: *He viewed 374 pages!*

I know what was going through my mind when I saw this, and it's probably the same thing that's going through your mind. Right now you're probably thinking, *What in the world??!*

There are a lot of assumptions you can make when you see that someone has viewed that amount of website content. You might be thinking to yourself, *My goodness! This man has way too much time on his hands!*

Or, *Geez, he must be a competitor!*

Or, *Maybe he has some sort of rare OCD disorder where he can't get enough information about swimming pools.*

In any case, I was very perplexed—and almost stunned—to learn just how much of our website content this individual had read.

But this isn't all. In fact, the story gets much more interesting. The same night that I discovered that Mr. G had read 374 pages of our site, I was continuing to look through the leads that came in when I noticed a lead from a lady named (Mrs.) G. It was easy to put two and two together and realize that Mr. G had a wife, who was also researching swimming pools.

What made this even funnier was that she had found us because she had been searching on Yahoo and typed in "Richmond, Virginia, swimming pools."

On top of that, she had read more than *140 pages* of the website herself.

Now, if you take these two individuals combined, *this couple had read more than five hundred pages of our site.*

Five hundred-plus pages . . . about fiberglass swimming pools.

The next day, I called Mr. G on the phone. He, of course, acted like he had known me for years, and quickly agreed to have me out to his house for a sales appointment.

Now, what do you suppose that sales appointment was like?

I will tell you. I walked into the house, and Mr. G was standing in his living room with a spreadsheet in his hands. On one side of the sheet was a model of the swimming pool that he was planning to buy, and on the other side of the sheet he had listed every option and accessory he was buying to go with the pool. Of course, all he needed from me was one little thing: the price.

I walked out of that appointment forty-five minutes later with a $5,000 deposit and a signed contract in my hands. As I drove away from the home, I started to laugh, as a thought occurred to me:

How much selling had I actually done that day?

The answer, of course, is *none*. The Gs weren't just 70 percent decided when I got there, they were more in the range of 99.9 percent decided that they were going to use our company.

Frankly, my only job on that day was "Don't screw this one up, pool guy." Thus, I laughed.

It turns out that Mr. G was not a freak, not a competitor, and not retired. Rather, he was a surgeon. But he was also a consumer—a consumer who, along with his wife, wanted to feel comfortable with a buying decision.

In fact, if you think about how you buy things, and how much research you do when you're serious about what you're buying, you'll see that you are likely grossly underestimating people's willingness to become comfortable with their buying decisions through the power of great, helpful information.

My appointment with the Gs was one of the last ones I ever went on as a pool guy. It was also easily one of the most powerful and memorable, because it taught me a clear lesson, one that I've seen time and time again, in multiple industries and businesses, all over the world:

Content—assuming it is honest and transparent—is the greatest sales tool in the world today.

29 | Content Never Sleeps

You may think that saying "Content—assuming it is honest and transparent—is the greatest sales tool in the world today" is too bold of a statement. You may even think, especially if you're clinging to the past, that it's simply not true. But let's look at it together for a moment.

I used to think I was really good at sales. In fact, I taught sales classes and achieved some very high performance numbers for years. But, as a human being, I am limited. Content, on the other hand, is not.

Here are some truths about content, especially the content on your website, assuming it's done right:

- Content can teach 1,000; 100,000; or even 1,000,000 people at a time. Its scope and reach have no limits. A salesperson, for the most part, can "teach" only those he or she is speaking in front of.
- Content never sleeps. It can work for you 24/7/365. It doesn't ask for holidays. It doesn't get sick. It simply keeps going.
- Content doesn't need a commission and never asks for a raise. It won't leave you for another company, and it will follow the rules and dictations you give it.
- A single piece of content can continue to work for you long after you've even forgotten about it. (Heck, many of the articles we've discussed here for River Pools are several years old, yet they generate hundreds of thousands of dollars each year in revenue. Essentially, they are "evergreen.")

131

Now, let me share some other telling statistics with you.

For years as a swimming pool salesman, my life was a total grind, consisting of incredible amounts of travel combined with sitting in front of home owners day in and day out. And considering the average sales appointment lasted two to three hours, combined with the fact that most appointments were more than two hours from my home, you can see why things were a little rough.

So as to add further perspective, in 2007, in order to sell 75 swimming pools, I had to go on roughly 250 sales appointments—a 30 percent closing ratio. That year, I worked well over sixty hours every week. Most nights I didn't get home until after 10 or 11 P.M. Time with my family was, for the most part, nonexistent.

I don't mention these things to give myself a pat on the back, I'm simply trying to set the stage to showcase the difference the principles in this book can make if you're willing to apply them to your business. I don't know about you, but having no life outside of driving and selling probably isn't the healthiest way to make a living, nor develop a powerful sales culture that's built to last within an organization.

Now, let's fast-forward to the point at which I started the process of assignment selling and integrating content throughout the sales process. In 2013, we sold 95 swimming pools, and in order to sell those 95 pools, we went on *120 sales appointments—a closing rate of 79 percent.*

When I share these statistics with other swimming pool companies, they do not believe we could ever sell that many swimming pools with that few appointments.

But here is the big key they are missing:

Guess how many pages, on average, those 95 customers in 2013 read? No, the answer is not 30.

It's not 50.

It's not even 80.

The answer, if you can believe it, was 105.

That's right, 95 customers, on average, were willing to read 105 pages of our website before they bought a swimming pool from our company.

And in 2016, the numbers are trending even higher.

To this day, despite having seen this same phenomenon in other industries with our clients, I'm still blown away with the results, as they're truly an astounding look at consumer behavior in the digital age.

You may be saying to yourself, *Marcus, how is that even possible?*

Well, if you had come to me seven years ago and asked, "Marcus, do you realize that swimming pool customers would be willing to read more than a hundred pages of your website before they buy?," I would have looked at you, called you a fool, and then proceeded to tell you that you were crazy and didn't understand my buyer, my customer, or my industry.

And I would have been dead wrong.

The sad reality is that, as some of you are reading these pages, you may still be thinking your industry and your business are different, and these principles don't apply to you. But I'm here to tell you that the principles are exactly the same.

Over the past few years, every client we have had at the Sales Lion who has initiated this process of They Ask, You Answer and become prolific teachers on their website has also discovered just how much content people (B2B and B2C) will view on their site before making a buying decision.

There are a few other points I'd like to make before closing this chapter.

I mentioned to you that we went on 120 sales calls to close 95 sales in 2013. I want you to think about that in terms of the impact on our salespeople. Instead of having to go on 250 sales appointments, our salespeople—who are arguably less skilled than I was all those years—now go on fewer than half that number; yet they have dramatically higher closing rates than I ever had.

In fact, let's do the math. Each sales appointment involves at least two hours driving each way plus two to three hours at the actual appointment. That means that each sales appointment involves a time expenditure of six to seven hours on average. So, if we go on 130 fewer appointments to achieve even better results, we have just saved more than eight hundred person-hours in a year.

What can one salesperson do with eight hundred additional hours in their year? The answers are obvious. They can:

- Spend a lot more time with qualified prospects and buyers
- Spend more time networking and focusing on business development
- And, most important, spend more time doing that which they love— be it with their family, friends, loved ones, hobbies, and so on. Frankly, that's what it's all about.

The moral of the story:

When you look at the power of content, it is not just about leads, traffic, and sales.

It is not just about building your brand, either.

It is about giving your company, your staff, and your salespeople more time. For time is the one thing that can never be recovered. Once it's gone, it's gone, and you will never be able to get it back. (I can personally attest to this, as I'm sure you can as well.)

If you can give this incredible gift (of time) to your employees, then not only do employee morale and overall culture improve, but you are making a serious impact on the world in the process.

30

Using Assignment Selling to Avoid Common Sales Pitfalls

Before we finish with assignment selling, I want to show you how you can use this sales strategy to avoid common sales pitfalls and mistakes.

Here's a very common sales scenario: A salesperson gives a prospect a proposal or a quote and a few days go by without hearing back from the prospect. As the days go by, the salesperson starts to get nervous, and they send the prospect an e-mail. That e-mail usually sounds something like this:

Hello, Mr./Mrs. Jones. We met a couple of days ago and I gave you a proposal. I'm just checking in to see if you have any questions. Don't hesitate to let me know. Sincerely, Salesperson.

That e-mail might as well be called a "Please-don't-break-up-with-me" letter because it essentially sounds like we're saying:

Dear Mr./Mrs. Jones, do you still love me? Yes or no? I sure hope you circled yes!

Almost everyone writes that type of e-mail when a prospect goes silent after receiving a proposal or quote. But it's completely ineffective.

It's at moments like this when it's easy to see the incredible power of assignment selling. Using the principles of assignment selling, your e-mail would consist of the following:

Hello, Mr./Mrs. Jones. We met a few days ago and I gave you a proposal. During our meeting, you mentioned a couple of questions and concerns you had. In order to further help you with these concerns, I've attached to this e-mail a video and an article that specifically address each. Please take a moment to give each a look, as I know they'll help you with this important decision. And tomorrow, I'll give you a call so we can discuss. Sincerely, Salesperson.

When we meet someone in a sales situation and give them our pitch or proposal, we generally believe we have properly addressed their concerns, and in the moment, we may have. But often, those same concerns will resurface after the prospect has some time to reflect upon our sales conversation or proposal.

So, instead of writing a "Please-don't-break-up-with-me" e-mail, writing an e-mail like the second one has two major benefits:

1. It will remind your prospect that they actually have nothing to worry about. You are offering the best solution to their problem. It reaffirms your expertise related to their particular concern.
2. It will force your prospect to respond in one of two ways:

They may respond with a simple "Thank you, this is great! It is exactly what I needed." When they respond in this manner, it is a clear sign that they are interested and things are looking very positive in terms of your ability to do business with that individual.

Conversely, they may respond by telling you they are not interested, and you are not a good fit for them. Knowing that you are going to contact them to ask about the homework you have now given them forces them to tell you the truth. As we've already discussed in this book: Time is your greatest asset in business and in life, and a candid answer like "I'm not interested" or "Actually, we've decided to go a different direction" saves you precious time.

You may be thinking right now that your business could not apply assignment selling to its sales process. I am here to tell you this is absolutely not the case.

In fact, each of the most successful clients we have worked with here at the Sales Lion, whether smaller companies or larger brands, have adopted this principle of using content in their sales process. Sure, it changes based on their product, service, buyer, sales cycle, and other factors, but the principle of using education to sell does not change.

31

Using Assignment Selling to Determine Compatibility

To give you a simple example close to home: Here at our digital sales and marketing agency, the Sales Lion, we also utilize an assignment selling process with our prospects. And keep in mind, our clients are other businesses, not consumers.

Because we get a very high number of leads coming into our system, we need to make sure that we're working with good fits and not bad fits. We want to make sure we're dealing with informed and educated clients versus those who really have no clue as to what we are and the services we provide—people who haven't done any research whatsoever.

In our case at the Sales Lion, we have a two hundred-page e-book entitled *Inbound and Content Marketing Made Easy*. Any prospect or company who approaches us through our site must read this e-book before they can have a conversation with me.

You may be wondering how we introduce this e-book to the prospect. Well, the prospect generally contacts us through a form on our website and says, "I would love to set up a phone consultation."

We then respond with an e-mail that looks something like this:

Hello, Mr./Mrs. Jones. Thank you so much for contacting us here at the Sales Lion. In your contact form, you requested a phone consultation with us. We certainly look forward to that conversation. But, in order to make it the most productive conversation for both parties, and in order to help you get the most out of the experience, we have attached an e-book for you to read before we speak. This e-book is the core of all our philosophy here at the Sales Lion. If you read this and feel good about what you see herein, you will know that we are a good fit for you as well as your needs. By the same token, if you read this and it does not align with your philosophies, you will also know if we are a bad fit for your current needs. Once you have completed the e-book, please respond to this e-mail so that we can set up a time to have our conversation. And, if you have already read the e-book, please just let me know and we will get that call set up right away. Sincerely, Marcus.

Let's talk about a couple of things you just read in that e-mail that make it unique:

- You will notice how the communication is based upon the principle that if the prospect does certain things, *they* will have a better experience. This is much more effective than saying, "Hey, Mr./Mrs. Jones, I really don't know if you're worth my time. In order to tell whether you are, please read this."
- The second principle that you will notice from that e-mail is the principle of disarmament, which we discussed in chapter 18. Here is how we have used disarmament with our prospect:
  - We have come right out and admitted that there is a chance that we will not be a good fit for them.
  - We have allowed the prospect to feel like they are in charge of identifying whether we are a good fit or not. But in reality, *we* are identifying whether they are a good fit for us.
  - We have allowed them to feel like they are in total control of their buying decision. The most successful salespeople in the world understand that one of the great keys to sales is helping the prospect feel like they are the ones making the buying decision. As human beings, we want to feel like we are in charge of our destiny and that nobody is telling us what to do.

Now, you may be thinking, *Marcus, there is no way somebody is going to read two hundred pages of an e-book before your initial conversation!*

I'm here to tell you that, once again, that is simply not the case. The only ones who are not willing to do this are the ones who are a bad fit for our company.

Look at it like this: If somebody reads two hundred pages of my words, my thoughts, my teachings, and my philosophy on sales and marketing, and then they come to me for a quote or proposal, they are unlikely to be also getting a bunch of other quotes because of a lack of confidence in me and my company.

The fact is, after reading two hundred pages of my teachings and philosophy, they either love me or hate me.

If they hate me, that's fine. We skip the phone conversation, acknowledge that it's a bad fit, and save each other time.

If they love me, it means I will have a much shorter sales cycle and a much more productive conversation with the prospect.

As you might imagine, the exact same thing is true with this book. There will be people who read this book and absolutely hate it. That's not a problem.

There will be another set who read it, want to apply its principles to their businesses (or vendors, conference, and the like) and contact me to discuss.

Assuredly, the sales cycle for those calls will not be very long. The work has already been done.

I have just given you two examples. One applies when you are selling a product and the other applies when you are selling a service.

I reiterate that we've worked with companies of all shapes and size that have made this work for them in their own way. A few key principles remain consistent, namely:

- Every e-mail sent out by your company's sales team is a teaching opportunity. So, stop sending out e-mails—especially e-mails of the sales variety—that do not include content that teaches the prospect or customer. It simply doesn't make sense.
- As you can see, your salespeople are the ones who are using the content in their sales process. If you are going to implement assignment selling

and use content in your company's sales process, the salespeople need to be informed and aware of the content that is being produced. In the following chapter, I talk about this very point and the incredible need for sales and marketing departments to become completely aligned into one unit, without silos.

32

Case Study 4

How a Start-Up Company in the Health Care Space Became the Thought Leaders of an Entirely New Industry

Many of the digital marketing success stories we've heard over the years have come from companies who got into it for very similar reasons: They wanted their voices to be heard above the clamorous din emitting from others in their industry. Many of these companies had to figure out a way to carve themselves a slice of the existing marketplace, and they used the principles of inbound marketing and They Ask, You Answer to do it.

Health Catalyst is unique in that it came into an industry that was still in its infancy—healthcare analytics. Started in 2010, Health Catalyst is a data warehousing, analytics, and outcomes improvement company that provides infrastructure that health care organizations (hospitals) can use to identify waste in their practices, allowing them to improve patient care and lower their overall costs.

In its new space, Health Catalyst quickly found that nobody was answering industry questions online. Despite that, some massive competitor

143

brands were also entering the space, no one was yet known as the thought leader of healthcare analytics.

Because of this, no real information existed online for interested searchers. Health Catalyst recognized there was a huge informational void in their industry, and they set out to fill it. Unlike with other businesses, Health Catalyst didn't have to fight to get their voice heard, because there were no other voices. Rather than push their way onto the stage, Health Catalyst was able to build the stage.

Paul Horstmeier, Health Catalyst senior vice president and former Hewlett-Packard vice president, was brought on board in 2012 when the company was ready to scale its sales and marketing efforts. Most of Health Catalyst's marketing up until that point had been through word-of-mouth referrals and press releases. Horstmeier was asked to start a marketing campaign nearly from scratch. Because he was a little rusty in heading a marketing department, Horstmeier started researching how companies were doing quality marketing.

I decided I needed to get up to speed with what was the latest and greatest in marketing. I started reading and looking at the concept of content marketing. I don't remember how, but I came across Marcus Sheridan's book, *Inbound and Content Marketing Made Easy*, and his philosophy (They Ask, You Answer) fit with what I already believed, so we had him come out for a workshop a few months later.

The base principles of They Ask, You Answer harmonized with Horstmeier's own philosophy of creating a culture in his industry based on educating the marketplace, rather than building a brand that simply sold a product and services.

I thought traditional marketing was dead. Most of the data that I had done in my research confirmed it. Only about 30 percent of people actually trust brands. So for the most part, you have to start from the perspective that nobody trusts what you're saying.

Paul Horstmeier had no trouble convincing his partners that the direction Health Catalyst needed to move in was to focus on properly educating the marketplace. Before the initial workshop even kicked off, Health

Catalyst already had top-to-bottom buy-in, a clear direction they wanted to take the company, and a new marketing team ready to carry out their new vision.

We were advocating something that was very new to the healthcare industry. We knew we needed to educate the market. When Marcus showed up and discussed his principles, it already fit into a paradigm that we believed. Doing the workshop with Marcus was the starting point of formally kicking off the process.

Phase 1: Uniting the Marketing and Sales Silos

Health Catalyst's first move was to implement the They Ask, You Answer methodology and draft up a list of the most common questions customers and clients ask. To get their list, the marketing team went to the sales team for answers. Horstmeier noticed that the senior sales teams were being pulled in multiple directions: as they were traveling to meet clients and potential prospects to explain their services. Horstmeier also noticed that the senior sales team were already the experts in the field and could better manage their efforts as part of the content production initiative.

It was pretty easy for me to say, "We're going to create a marketing engine, and it's going to be all about education, and if you participate, it will relieve you of travel and reduce the demand on you. Because I'm going to create two ways, one via publishing and the other via webinars, to get your content out to thousands of people instead of tens of people."

It was so easy to catch the vision. We were fortunate in that the subject matter experts that we had on our team were the subject matter experts nationally. We were in a new market and we were already the thought leaders, and we were already in demand.

For their first phase of content marketing, Horstmeier and his marketing crew leveraged the knowledge of their sales team to write compelling articles. However, after a few months of utilizing the sales experts and doing their own independent research, the marketing team surpassed the sales team as the thought leaders and relied less heavily on sales for content ideas.

Health Catalyst began to churn out three pieces of content each week, and in an industry nearly devoid of information, getting to the top of the first page on searches came pretty easily for the company.

We have about seventy-seven strategic keyword phrases that we target, and we own almost all of them. We have three segments of keywords. In our first segment, we have 95 percent of our words at the number 1 spot. In our two other segments we're at 50 percent. We have 100 percent of all the words on the first page of Google search engine results, with 50 percent of our words at the top position.

Another reason Health Catalyst's efforts have been so amazing is the way they have broken down the barrier between sales and marketing so that everyone is on board with the production and distribution of content. And it's not just *that* their sales team uses their content, but the *way* they do it. Says Horstmeier:

Our content team has grown. I have a core team, and I have a separate team that just writes "case studies." The sales team particularly uses the case studies. I've also created a tool on our website called "My Folder." This tool allows anyone (but the sales team uses it the most) to go onto our website, sort through whatever articles, case studies, or information they're looking for to give to a client and put those things in the "My Folder" tool. The salesperson can then send any file they add to the folder to a client. An automatic e-mail is generated saying, "Hey, George, thank you very much for the meeting that we had. You asked for more info on XYZ. I've identified the three most important pieces of content I'd like you to read. Take a look and let me know what you think."

Phases 2 and 3: Live Webinars and Events

Producing regular content on their site was working very well for Health Catalyst but they still knew there was more they could be doing to educate the marketplace. Educating clients was extremely important to Health Catalyst. One the one hand, having all the information helped their sales team get new clients. On the other hand, Health Catalyst's product is pretty technical, and adequately getting their clients to purchase and use the product required making sure the people using it were using it correctly.

For phase 2 of Health Catalyst's marketing strategy they began to implement regular live webinars for their clients, prospects, and anybody interested to attend their training sessions. All the webinars are free, and many have been recorded, and topics a person may be interested in are always available. Says Horstmeier:

> What's pretty interesting about webinars is that everyone told us that in the health care industry the only way webinars would work is if we were featuring clients and not ourselves. But I knew that we had the thought leaders within our company. So we had a meeting and decided that our webinars would have a "content marketing mind-set," in which it would be all about educating and teaching. We didn't want to mention our company name much, if at all, because we try to teach principles and broaden the appeal of what we do.

Health Catalyst's education-over-promotion approach to webinars has paid off in a remarkable way with an average sign-up for webinars between 600 and 700 people and as many as 1,200 people attending a single session.

In phase 3, Health Catalyst's created an industry event. One of the concerns that Horstmeier had about doing events was that, as a vendor and not a third party, hosting an event might come off as too promotional and not enough about educating the marketplace. Horstmeier agreed to host a healthcare analytics summit under one very strict guideline: to make sure it's an educational summit and not a Health Catalyst vendor event.

> The only mention during the whole summit of Health Catalyst was a small logo that said "powered by Health Catalyst." Unless you were really looking, you'd miss it. We were so committed to making it an analytics event and not a sponsored event that we asked everyone at the very end to vote if they thought it was a vendor event or an analytics event. Ninety-four percent of the people voted that we had kept our promise of making it about analytics and not Health Catalyst.

The transparency of their motives and their pledge to cultivate a culture instead of building a brand has made them the trusted thought leaders in their space. When Health Catalyst hosted its first analytics summit, the expected attendance was between 100 to 250, and 620 people showed. Their second annual summit surpassed expectations once again.

> We just finished our second healthcare analytics summit. We widely expanded it. We had a capacity of 1,000 people, and we sold out six weeks ahead of time. We had to get approval to host any more people, so we ended up having 1,040 people there with 180 on the waiting list. And that was our second year.

Success and Plans for the Future

Health Catalyst's efforts have not only put them on the map, but they've also made them an industry thought leader. They built a marketing strategy based on education, teaching, and transparency that transformed into a culture. And others in their field have taken notice. Says Horstmeier:

> We've had several analysts give us an overall market review of our company, and they always put us at the top of the list. We had another analyst tell us that Health Catalyst's marketing was the most brilliant marketing campaign she'd ever seen in the industry. Our own president said, "In my twenty-five years in the health care field, I've never seen anything like this." Our clients are coming and they're already educated. We walk into a meeting and they already know what we're doing. They've read our stuff. They've already asked questions. Many of them are ready to buy by the time we have our first meeting.

In just a little over two years, traffic to Health Catalyst's website has grown exponentially from a few thousand monthly visitors in August 2013 to more than 115,000 in October 2015, with most of the increase coming organically from solid search engine optimization (SEO) practices.

> Right now it's hard to measure the ROI [return on investment] of our marketing efforts as we average a 12- to 18-month sales cycle. Our average sale is probably 2½ to 3 million dollars and our company has a total of 30 clients. The other thing that makes it difficult to measure is that there isn't always one thing that creates a lead. It's always a combination of things. We have content, webinars, events, and people coming to our

website saying "Tell me more." So depending on what you'd consider a lead, we're getting about 200 inquiries per quarter. When we tracked the percentage of leads that came through the marketing engine it was 60 to 70 percent of all leads coming through.

The Health Catalyst story is the ultimate example of a B2B industry where, instead of saying, "Hospitals don't find vendors on the Internet," the organization embraced the idea that an obsession with education and transparency—in all its forms—could have a dramatic impact on the brand and business.

And boy did it have an impact.

PART III

Implementation and Making It a Culture

Many companies have tried content marketing and failed.

Having spoken to so many companies on this subject, I've heard just about all the reasons why such failures occur. And not only that, but my consulting company has worked with dozens and dozens of businesses and brands to help them achieve greatness within their space.

Some have reached incredible heights of success.

Others have been a total bust.

As we've taken the time to separate the success stories from the busts, we've discovered there are four essential keys to making this work within any organization: ultimately building the business, brand, and bottom line while becoming a true culture in the process. And in this part of the book, we break down these four keys, which are as follows:

1. *Buy-in from top to bottom*: This is achieved through truly educating subject matter experts and key departments on the *what, how,* and *why* of content marketing.
2. *Insourcing*: The process of utilizing company employees to produce content as part of their job descriptions.
3. *The content manager*: Someone in the organization must own the effort and be fully dedicated to it (without distractions) to make it work.
4. *Using the right tools*: Unless the right tools are used, it is extremely hard to calculate true ROI (return on investment) of the company's content marketing efforts.

33 | The Power of Insourcing and Using Your Team to Create Incredible Content

Truth be told, many, many organizations have tried embracing inbound and content marketing. And one of the most common ways they do this is by engaging some type of digital marketing agency that produces their content for them. Although this concept of "outsourcing" your company's content production is by no means a bad thing, it can absolutely come with drawbacks. Here's why:

1. For the most part, unless the content producer (for the agency) is embedded in the company, it is very difficult for them to accurately reflect you, your brand, your brand story, and the subject matter expertise your company has. In many ways, your company's content and story represent the soul of your business. This being the case, it can be quite difficult for someone else to accurately reflect this "soul."

2. Agencies have a set "deliverable." For example, many may include something like "six blog articles a month" as part of the scope of work. On one hand, this is a very good thing because you know, as the client, that you're going to get six blog articles that month to publish to the site. But on the other hand, the companies that have had the greatest success following the principles of They Ask, You Answer and content marketing generally aren't restricted by deliverables. In other words:

   - If they want to produce ten blog articles in a month, they do it.
   - If they want to create twelve videos in a month, they do it.
   - If they want to write just one, epically long and valuable blog post, they do it.
   - If they want to revamp a portion of their website to better address buyer needs and concerns, they do it.

I hope you're seeing the point here. The creative flexibility to simply produce great content, in all its forms, without the limitations of a contract or deliverable, is a powerful, powerful thing.

3. Finally, when a company is not dependent on an agency to "do the work for it," and therefore learn it for itself, although the learning curve can mean slower results at first, the end results are often dramatically greater.

4. It's critical that your company's story and content are a true reflection of your sales messaging. This means, in a perfect world, that your sales team is very much involved in the selection and production of all of your company and brand content (more on this later). Done right, when a prospect or customer contacts you, their first thought is *Yes, this is exactly who I thought they were. What they are saying is exactly what I read and saw.*

Ultimately, the question of producing your own content versus having someone else do it for you is much like the principle of the artist: Not until the artist is holding her own paintbrush can she truly produce her own masterpiece. The same is true for any company looking to become a thought leader in the digital age.

I stress again that there are many great agencies out there that do produce great content. There are also many great ghost writers. But the fact remains, if you want to be heard above the noise of your industry, you can't just be average. You can't be like everyone else in your space. You must do more, and you must do it better.

Thus, owning your content effort, versus renting it out, can make all the difference.

All of this leads to the opposite of outsourcing your company's content, something we call at the Sales Lion "insourcing," which we define as:

The process of using your existing employees and their knowledge about your services and products to produce educational content for the marketing department—leading to better, buyer-centric content, more informed sales teams, and dramatically increased brand awareness.

34 | How Block Imaging Embraced a Culture of Insourcing

If you read the foreword of this book, you're familiar with the story of Block Imaging and Krista Kotrla. Krista wanted badly to turn Block Imaging around and knew that the principles of They Ask, You Answer would be the key not only to saving the business, but to making them the leader of the medical imaging equipment space in the process.

But when she approached the sales and leadership departments of her organization, no one seemed to share her vision. The excuse? It was twofold:

1. "I don't have the time."
2. "That's not my job."

Let's look at both of these excuses for a second. In life, when someone tells you they "don't have time," what they're really trying to tell you, without actually telling you is, "That thing you just explained to me is not as important to me as it is to you."

In other words, they don't see its value.

The funny thing is, whenever we as humans or businesses see the value of something, we quickly start to make the time. In fact, "time" becomes a non-issue when profit and worth are identified.

The excuse of "That's not my job" is essentially the same. In 2016, if someone within an organization tells their marketing department, "It's not my job," they obviously don't understand what has happened with the shifts in sales and marketing in the digital age. They don't understand the 70 percent number we discussed at the beginning of this book and just how much the buyer's journey has changed.

Again, they don't get it.

In Krista's case, neither management nor the sales department at Block Imaging understood the value of this incredibly important philosophy. Without question, though, the story of marketing departments not getting help from the rest of the team is prolific throughout the entire world today. And when I say "prolific," I am not exaggerating. In fact, since starting the Sales Lion, the number 1 e-mail I have received from readers—and it's number 1 by a longshot—sounds something like this:

Marcus, I am in marketing. I believe so much in using this honest, transparent teaching philosophy in doing business. But I just can't get management and sales to see what I see!

I have received hundreds of these types of e-mails over the years, and the frustration from the sender is almost always palpable.

The Silos Must Be Eliminated

Krista's dilemma is the same one shared by most people in marketing: they understand their products, services, and buyer, they just don't understand them the same way sales or management does. Simply put, they are not (generally speaking) subject matter experts. After all, it's the sales teams (among others in the organization) that hear all of the main prospect and customer questions. It's also the same sales team that is tasked with answering these questions.

So if sales is on the front lines, why would they not be included in the part of the sales process that has the greatest impact on the sale? The idea that we can simply tell marketing, "Go and produce this content. Get us lots of leads. Move prospects down the funnel" is utterly ridiculous and outrageously improbable.

Understanding the *What, How,* and *Why*

When Krista asked me to come and speak to her company, and help the various departments catch the vision that was inbound, content, and They Ask, You Answer, I knew it was a tremendous opportunity, for myself and also for their team.

For the team because they would all be in a room, with their full focus and attention on understanding the *what, how,* and *why* of becoming the best teachers and educators in the medical imaging space.

For me because that was the first time I would go out and teach such a workshop—one focused on developing a true "culture" of content marketing. Because I could see the workshop was going to have such an influence on Krista's team, and because I knew so many other "Kristas" who were out there struggling to achieve the same type of uniform vision and buy-in she was seeking, I knew that my days of being a pool guy were numbered.

Since that day, I've taught hundreds of these same workshops around the globe, and the results have been extraordinary. But the key to making them so effective comes down to three simple things:

1. What is this thing we call content marketing?
2. How does it work (They Ask, You Answer)?
3. Why is it so very important that everybody in the company participate in it?

Since that day with Block Imaging, Krista has had the help of well over fifty employees who have contributed to producing hundreds of articles, videos, and so on that have gone on the company website. But it all happened because they understood one key thing:

Everyone is a teacher, and everyone's voice matters.

When companies think this way, anything is possible. The marketing department changes. So does sales. Silos are eliminated. Culture and teamwork are enhanced.

And just to help you really catch the vision of what is possible when things are done this way, read the following e-mail Krista received from one of her sales team members in early 2016, five years after the original workshop:

Guys,

Y'all may be sick of hearing these stories, but I still get a kick out of it. I just had a conference call with a pain management center in Arkansas. Come to find out before we even spoke, the purchaser had printed off several of my blogs to bring to her board meeting. It enabled her to answer questions on comparison models, budgets, what equipment they needed, etc.

She had read and seen so much of our content, she said she couldn't wait to talk to me. She told me who my competitors were and how much they were quoting. Even when I told her we would likely charge more, she said, "but I trust you guys, I'd rather work with you."

I realize they don't all line up like this, but when our funnel is working at its best it is so so so sweet. . . . I'm sure I could still find a way to screw up the deal, but the point is, I couldn't be better set up to succeed.

The effort to produce the content is WORTH IT! Thank you to the stellar efforts of the marketing team for really setting us apart.

Think about it, when was the last time your sales team sent an e-mail to the marketing department that looked like this?

To close this chapter, here is a direct quote from Krista, speaking on the final results of They Ask, You Answer for Block Imaging:

"Because of Insourcing and Content Marketing, we can account for at least 20 million in sales we otherwise would never have gotten."

35

Starting Off They Ask, You Answer with a Bang

Company Workshops

I hope that by this point you're excited about They Ask, You Answer.

You want your organization and brand to be seen as the most trusted thought leader of your space.

You want to embrace insourcing and involve your team of subject matter experts.

You want this to be a culture.

All this being said, cultures aren't built on e-mails, announcements, and mission statements.

As you might imagine, if you finish this book, set it down, and then send out an e-mail to your team that says, "Let's start answering customer questions and blogging," you will likely get nowhere quickly.

Again, your team must understand the *what*, *how*, and *why* of They Ask, You Answer so as to allow what is a "program" in many people's eyes to eventually become a culture.

This is exactly why workshops (as well as long-term training) with the entire team are so critical to success. With every single business and brand

I've worked with that has experienced exceptional results, a workshop has always been the key to kicking off the magic and creating a unified vision.

I discovered this first with Krista and her team at Block Imaging; I have since witnessed it well over two hundred times in the workshops I've taught to organizations, large and small, over the past five years.

But if you want to give a workshop to help your team catch this vision, what is the best way to go about it? What are the key principles to focus on? What must the team clearly understand in order to get started?

In this chapter, we answer these questions by showing you the eight essential principles participants must embrace from the very beginning so as to find the greatest success with content marketing and They Ask, You Answer—principles that are ideally taught in a workshop designed to lay out the entire vision of the content marketing efforts.

Principle 1: Consumer Expectations Have Changed

In this section of the workshop, the purpose is to shift the mind of each attendee into "consumer" mode. In other words, we want them thinking about the way *they* use the Internet, how *their expectations* have changed when *they* are researching and vetting companies online, and the feelings *they* experience when a website doesn't give them what they're looking for.

Unless someone has the ability to look in the mirror and analyze the way they shop, buy, and engage the Web, it's very difficult for them to understand their prospects and customers at the level necessary.

Principle 2: The Way Google and Other Search Engines Work

Here's a little secret: Outside of the tech/marketing world, *a huge portion of people do not understand how search engines work.* Nor can they articulate how and why Google ranks and shows some sites (pieces of content) over others.

Ultimately, the key to this section of the workshop is to help every person realize *the goal of Google (and other search engines) is to give its customer (the searcher) the best, most specific answer to their question (or need, problem, query, and so on) in that very moment.* At the same time, even though Google wants to give great answers to their customers, most companies and industries don't embrace this "teacher" mentality online, leaving the reward to third-party websites that are more driven by consumer questions than by product pitches.

Principle 3: The Way Consumers Search and the Big 5

In the first part of the book, we discussed the critical nature of the Big 5 and how it drives consumer research around the world:

1. Pricing and Costs
2. Problems
3. Versus and Comparisons
4. Reviews
5. Best in Class

The key to this section of the workshop is to help your team members reflect on all the times they've used each one of these phrases as keywords while they were shopping or researching online. When done correctly, everyone in the room will be nodding their head again and again once they realize just how often they use the Big 5 in every aspect of their consumer-driven life. By coming to this understanding, they'll also start to see how the Big 5 greatly apply to *their* existing prospects and customers.

If your organization is going to have great success with this, you cannot compromise in your desire to address all consumer questions. Regardless of how good, bad, or ugly the question may appear, if the marketplace is asking it, you must address it. And your team must share this vision of wanting to address it versus retreating back to the old way of burying their heads in the sand, hoping the prospect never asks the question (ostrich marketing).

Principle 4: Group Brainstorm of Content Ideas

In this section of the workshop, the goal is to answer this question: *What should we write about?*

Instead of making it a science, the key comes down to listening well, hearing the problems, questions, and needs of prospects and customers, and then having a willingness to address each one (be it via text, video, or other medium).

Now that attendees understand the They Ask, You Answer philosophy, as well as how this coordinates so perfectly with the Big 5, the next step is to have them apply what they've learned by brainstorming questions they receive every day from prospects and clients.

This activity can have a profound impact on all participants, and as you might imagine, it's usually dominated by those persons involved in sales, because they are the ones who generally have the closest contact with existing and potential customers.

Principle 5: The Impact Content Can Have on the Sales Process and Closing Rates

Remember earlier when we said, "Employees need to understand 'why' they're being asked to participate in content marketing?" Well, this section is a *huge* deal. As with everything else in life, people want to know WIIFT: *What's In It For Them.*

By seeing the dramatic impact great content can have on shortening the sales cycle while bringing in more qualified leads and greater margins, salespeople are generally *very* excited about the possibilities this could have on their bottom line and overall job performance.

Principle 6: The Reason Why Everyone's Voice, Talents, and Knowledge Are Critical for Success

The essence of principle 6 is very simple: *Marketing should not be the digital voice of the company.* Marketing does not have its finger on the pulse of clients and customers like the rest of the company. Therefore, marketing's job (from this point forward) is to help employees (who deal with customers or are subject matter experts) produce content (and therefore earn trust).

Essentially, upon hearing this, each branch of the business needs to understand its overall value to the growth of the company, and why it's critical that the marketing department is able to lean on them for teaching, information, and other pieces of content.

Principle 7: The Editorial Guidelines Going Forward

If employees are going to participate in the company's content marketing efforts, they'll need to understand what the entire process and corresponding expectations look like. Here are just a few questions and topics that should be covered:

- Who is the person in charge? (The title of this position varies, be it content manger, chief content officer, or other label.)
- How often will employees be asked to contribute content, and how often will they be required to meet with someone in marketing to produce said content?
- What are the different ways in which the employees will be able to contribute content? (text, video, or other media)
- What are the editorial guidelines for a typical blog post?

After employees are done with this section of the workshop, they should have a clear road map in their heads of next steps, their individual roles, and expectations going forward.

Principle 8: A Look into the Future

This section recaps everything that has been covered in the workshop up to this point, including the benefits to the company as a whole and to each employee as well. Also, we have found that a very powerful discussion point in this section can be achieved by asking this simple question:

What would prevent this culture of content marketing from working in our organization?

I hope that this section has given you a better sense of what needs to be understood from Day 1 to make the most out of They Ask, You Answer and establish a true culture of content marketing. Keep in mind, too, that all of what is being stated here is flexible and can be adjusted to meet the needs of your company or organization.

But the key, as always, is that *it happens.* Otherwise, resistance is likely on the horizon.

36

The Content Manager Qualities, Hiring, and More

I hope that by this point in the book you're getting a simple impression: "I need to do this."

And if that's the impression you're getting, great, you're already on the way to becoming the most trusted voice and expert within your space.

But at the same time, to make all of this possible, it's more than just having the right strategy or getting the buy-in of your sales team.

Embracing content marketing and the philosophies of They Ask, You Answer is a big task, and unless someone owns it, it's very likely *not* going to work.

This "owner" can go by many names within an organization (especially based on how large the company is), such as:

- Chief content officer
- Content marketing manager
- Content manager
- Chief storyteller
- Brand journalist
- Inbound marketing manager
- And so on

Ultimately, though, the name isn't what matters.

The thing that does matter, though, is that he or she exists within the organization.

Often, upon speaking to a marketer or CEO about turning content marketing into a culture, I'll have a conversation that sounds something like this:

MARKETING PERSON/CEO: I know we should be doing content marketing and following They Ask, You Answer. But I'm simply wearing too many other hats, and there is no way I can make the time for this myself.

ME: You need a content manager. Someone must *own* this effort and dedicate all their time to it, assuming you truly want to get exceptional results. (And for a larger organization, multiple content managers and editors should be dedicated to these efforts.)

MARKETING PERSON/CEO: I agree, but I think I can at least do some of this myself.

ME: Well, to be frank, you can't. At least, you won't do it very well. It will always play second fiddle to your other roles. I've seen it too many times.

MARKETING PERSON/CEO: But I'm just not sure the company is willing/able/ready/and so on to make this type of hire.

ME: And if you don't, again, it very likely won't work. Either you do this right or don't do it at all. You wearing another hat is only going to cause you more stress and produce little results . . . and that will lead to your team making false statements like, "We tried this content marketing stuff, but it didn't work for us."

I've had this very same conversation hundreds of times over the years, yet it keeps coming back again and again.

Someone Must Own It

Fact is, most businesses would rather dip their toes in the content marketing waters before they dive in. I get that. It's tempting. But just because something is tempting doesn't make it a good idea.

Here at The Sales Lion, as you've seen by the various case studies throughout this book, we've been blessed to watch many of our clients have some exceptional success stories. But for all of these success stories, there is one commonality:

Producing great content is a full-time job, and someone has to own it.

And whenever we've allowed our clients to try this strategy without a true "owner" of the content marketing, it hasn't worked out. Other priorities always took precedence. Production was too slow. The entire team never caught the vision.

But if we're being honest with ourselves, at this point in the game, knowing just how much the consumers and the buying process have changed, how could anyone deny the need to give the digital side of their business full attention?

Duties of a Content Manager (per Week)

To better understand why this is a full-time position for at least one person (depending on the organization's size), let's look at what a typical week looks like for an effective content manager.

With most of our clients, regardless of the size of their businesses, a "successful" week of content marketing will look like this:

- At least three new pieces of content (be it text, video, or audio): **5–15 hours**
- Company e-mail marketing efforts: **1–3 hours**
- Site analytics, SEO, and so on: **3–5 hours**
- Social media engagement: **1–2 hours**
- Premium content production (e-books, white papers, webinars, and so on): **3–5 hours**
- General website enhancements (new pages, call-to-action placement, and so on): **2–4 hours**
- Continual education/training (Learning tools like HubSpot, new apps, and so on): **3–5 hours**
- Meeting with the sales team to discuss needed content, have trainings, and so on: **2–4 hours**

Note: Depending on the organization, the industry, the customer base, and so on, all of these numbers can wildly vary. In this example, they are simply meant to give the reader a sense of the various responsibilities of a true content manager.

There are, of course, other duties that will require one's time, but my hope is you see just how quickly all these duties add up. And for larger organizations, it's easy to fill these same tasks with multiple employees. For example, many of our clients not only have a content manager, but also a full-time videographer, full-time writers, and more.

And for each, the return on the investment of these positions has been more than worth it.

Choosing the Right Leader of Your Content Marketing Efforts

Let's assume you're ready to go all-in with content marketing and embrace the philosophy of They Ask, You Answer. Now that you're ready to hire a content manager, you must make sure that the hire is good. And when I say "good," I mean really, really good.

But what defines *good* in this case? What skill sets should you be looking for, especially when you're seeking to fill this position within your company? Here are what we have found to be the ten essential qualities of every successful content marketing manager (CMM); a list we use every time my team is tasked with hiring a CMM for an organization.

Ten Essential Qualities of Great Content Marketing Managers

1. *They love to write.* This one goes without saying, but it's a *big* deal. And remember, writing online isn't just about fancy words. It's about *clean communication*, done in a way so that just about any reader can understand what's being said. Remember, great writers and communicators (and teachers) don't try to sound smart, which is never the goal of content marketing. Rather, they seek "communion," and it's this quality that makes them great.

Furthermore, if the individual loves writing, it also means he or she is fast, effective, and able to meet writing deadlines.

Without question, this skill is non-negotiable. Plus, you must remember this key:

You can always teach a great writer to be a good marketer, but you can't always teach a good marketer to be a great writer.

2. *They are skilled at editing.* When companies leverage their existing employees to produce textual and video content (insourcing), the initial product can at times be "rough." But great content managers can take what is a 5 in terms of quality and make it a 9 or 10—doing their best to make the original source as clear and concise as possible for the reader.

Note: Within a larger organization, this person would be considered an editor, but at the beginning, most content managers wear multiple hats, this being one of them.

3. *They have excellent interviewing skills.* This is *huge.* Any legitimate company or organization is full of subject matter experts, but most of these same experts are not great writers and certainly not great content marketers.

Because insourcing is so critical to success, a great content marketing manager understands how to sit down with these people (and vendors as well) and ask the right questions to stimulate content that teaches, helps, and informs readers.

Furthermore, they can ask the questions from the consumer's or buyer's point of view—which is the absolute key to creating communion, understanding, and trust between buyers and businesses—the feeling of being "understood."

4. *They embrace social media and "get it."* It goes without saying that social media—in some form or another—is here to stay. Therefore, the mind-set of "I don't like social media" isn't necessarily the best one for a content marketing manager to have. In fact, it's a bad sign. Granted, social media, as discussed herein, isn't something every company should focus on, but they should be at least open and accepting of the possibilities.

5. *They have solid video editing skills.* Video just keeps getting bigger and bigger and bigger. In fact, for many of our clients at the Sales Lion, *video is way more important than text* when producing a heavy amount of content while attempting to utilize employees—especially those persons in the sales department.

In a perfect world, once the company is of any size, a full-time videographer will be hired to show the visual story of the company. But until that point, the content manager should have the ability to wear both hats, and with the ease of making, creating, and editing videos today, this is absolutely achievable.

6. *They are extremely likeable.* Do you remember the amazing success story of Krista Kotrla and Block Imaging? Well, among the many reasons Krista was so effective in exploding Block Imaging's brand and bottom

line, her likeability was a major factor. Her company's employees love her. She brightens up their day, she has their respect, and because of this, they are quick to help with content marketing.

Frankly, when it comes down to it, unlikeable people make *awful* content marketing managers.

7. *They understand what makes people tick.* Again, when using employees as sources of content, knowing how to get said employees motivated and inspired is critical. This is exactly why the best content managers know how to push the right buttons to give their employees the needed boost to contribute to the company's marketing and sales goals.

8. *They are organized and goal oriented.* Content marketing, especially when done in businesses of any size, needs to have *order*. This starts with a main editorial calendar and continues with newsletters, trainings, interviews, and so on. All of these elements require order, planning, and organization.

9. *They love analytics, numbers, and measurement.* As I've worked closely with so many CEOs and marketers on their content marketing over the past few years, I keep seeing a simple trend:

Those persons who pay attention to the numbers get *wayyyyy* more results.

This is another reason why a content marketing manager eventually needs to be skilled not just with Google Analytics, but also with other tools, like HubSpot, Infusionsoft, and others.

10. *They are continually thinking outside the box.* Look around at the greatest content marketing examples and I'll show you creativity and unique thinking every time. Fact is, the best ones in this industry aren't looking for a set of rules or a road map that tells them exactly what they need to do next.

Instead, *they just get stuff done,* however they possibly can, and often with some serious creativity acting as the catalyst to success.

Why a Trained Journalist May Be a Perfect Match for Your Content Marketing Needs

As you look at these ten qualities, it's pretty obvious why the journalism industry has taken content marketing by storm. In fact, at my company, the Sales Lion, almost all of our hires for content marketing managers for our clients come directly from this industry; the majority are recent

journalism graduates, ready for work, and perfectly suited to meet this position's demands at a very reasonable price. Granted, they absolutely do need
to get the necessary training to "think like a marketer" and embrace the
philosophy of They Ask, You Answer, but there is no question, assuming
they are good, they can get the job done.

With so much of this talent available (because of the dying newspaper
industry), there is really no excuse for companies not to fill this position
and start receiving the benefits to their business, brand, and bottom line
immediately.

Also, keep in mind that as I write this, I fully realize not every company
can afford to hire a full-time content manager. I was a perfect example of
that with River Pools and Spas, when I embraced They Ask, You Answer in
2009. But it was for that very reason I worked at my kitchen table producing
content almost every single night from 10 P.M. to 1 A.M. for two straight years.

In my case, I didn't have a choice. But knowing what I know now and
seeing what I've seen, if you do have a choice, get the right people in the
rights seats from the beginning.

Finally, you may be asking what specific tests you can use to choose the
right content manager during the hiring process.

Again, because we've done so much of this at the Sales Lion, we have
found certain activities to be very effective, as well as a few things you
should be paying close attention to.

How Do You Ensure the Candidate Is a Match for the Organization And Brand?

I *really* emphasize finding someone who totally embodies your top five
organizational values. They are going to be writing on behalf of the
brand "voice," so you want it to be an effortless, one-and-the-same brand
personality.

You might give potential candidates perform the following exercises
during the vetting and hiring process:

- Ask them to turn a really poorly written rough draft into a nice article.
- Give them only an outline of an article and ask them to turn it into two
  full-blown articles.

- Give them a list of blog titles and have them write the interview questions they would use to interview an expert to complete the article.
- Give them a "question" that acts as the main subject of a video or blog post. Now, instead of you interviewing them, have them interview you (either in front of the camera or simply by taking notes) so as to get a full and thorough answer for said question. Once the interview is done, give the candidate a short window (24–48 hours) to return with a completed blog post (or video) answering said question.

As you might imagine, this final activity is extremely effective because it tests the candidate on multiple fronts: Their abilities to interview well, think on her feet, ask great question, meet deadlines, and produce solid content.

I also suggest having several people from your team interview the candidate just to make sure they are likable and get along well with everyone.

And finally, make note of their personal interests. Do they write for fun? Are they into producing their own videos? Do they consistently use social media as well? Do they have creative hobbies? Do you sense they are called to create and grow something of their own?

Remember, the tools and the strategy can be taught. The values, curiosity, and natural passion for both people and writing are critical to making all of this come together and ultimately to get greatness.

37

On the Importance of Tools

Measuring Return on Investment, the Power of HubSpot, and More

As we've established throughout this book, They Ask, You Answer is a business philosophy that guides the sales and marketing approach of an organization through obsessive listening, teaching, and a desire to solve the problems of the marketplace.

And in order for this philosophy to work, a few things have to happen.

- There must be shared buy-in.
- Departments must be aligned.
- Everyone needs to understand the underlying vision.
- Great, quality-driven content needs to be produced through text, audio, video, and other media.

But after all of this is done, it's critical that a business can answer the following question:

But did it make us any money?

If your organization is going to spend the time, resources, and money needed to make content marketing and They Ask, You Answer work, there absolutely should be an ongoing understanding of the company's return on investment (ROI).

And in case you hadn't noticed, the principle of showing ROI has been a major part of this book and the case studies herein.

Whether it was the "How Much Does a Fiberglass Pool Cost?" article that generated more than 3 million in revenue for River Pools, or Krista's statement of "20 million in additional revenue" with Block Imaging—the numbers have been a major part of the discussion, as well they should be.

You see, the fact is, as businesses, *we must make money.*

And then we must turn a profit.

All this They Ask, You Answer stuff is nice, but without it helping you to seriously generate more revenue for your company, it's not worth the price tag on the cover.

It is for this reason that, with digital marketing and sales, tools do matter—a lot.

When I was a struggling pool guy on the brink of losing my business in early 2009, I spent quite a bit of time reading about digital marketing and how such things as content marketing, blogging, and so on could make such a big difference on a business's bottom line. And although I found many helpful websites during this time period, the one place I kept going back to again and again was a start-up "marketing automation" software called HubSpot.

Since the early days when I was learning from the company, HubSpot has become somewhat famous in the world of marketing for a phrase their two founders—Brian Halligan and Dharmesh Shah—championed from the beginning of the company: "inbound marketing."

As they explained it to me in 2009, this "inbound" marketing was essentially the opposite of old-school "outbound" marketing. It was about providing value (through information) to consumers online, leading them to come to you (inbound) versus the traditional method of bombarding consumers with interruption-based content like TV, radio, print advertising, and so on.

For me, the message was obvious and something we needed to do, which is exactly why we ended up embracing our They Ask, You Answer philosophy.

But because they had done so much to educate me on the way inbound marketing worked, HubSpot had gained my trust. And because they'd gained it, the idea of using their software to measure our success and enhance our inbound efforts only made sense.

So despite the fact that we didn't have the money to pay for it, we signed up for HubSpot in March 2009.

Since that time, the impact HubSpot has had on River Pools and Spas, as well as our clients at the Sales Lion, has been phenomenal. Specifically, here we discuss the four major benefits we've encountered, benefits that every business must consider if they truly want to reach their online potential:

1. The ability to measure ROI
2. The ability to track lead behavior
3. The ability to track SEO
4. The ability to test your website

1. The Continuous Ability to Measure ROI of Your Digital Marketing Efforts

This is a big, big deal. As mentioned, if you're going to embrace content marketing and They Ask, You Answer—and spend the time/effort/money/and so on to make it work—you need to see returns. And when I say "returns," I'm not just talking about visitors or leads to your website. We're talking sales and revenue.

By using a tool like HubSpot, whenever anyone on your website fills out a form (contact form, e-book download form, and so on), you have the ability to "track" that person (or, specifically, his or her IP address). With this tracking, you're able to see to major data points that will allow you to measure ROI: the first page of the site they landed on and how they got there in the first place.

The reason why first-page-landed-on is so important is that, if someone is using a search engine like Google, lands on that page, and then eventually goes so far as to become a customer—you can now trace the customer's first visit to the website back to that page, therefore giving that singular page credit for the sale and revenue numbers.

It is for this reason I was able to say in chapter 11 that one article, "How Much Does a Fiberglass Pool Cost?," generated our company more than $3,000,000 in revenue. It is also for this reason every case study you've read up to this point has done the same—showing true revenue numbers as the ROI.

Aside from first page viewed, the other factor that's critical in measuring ROI is knowing what website (or means) brought the visitor to the website.

For example, many companies today use pay per click (PPC) advertising (like Google AdWords) to generate traffic to their websites. Whenever I'm discussing this subject with a company and they tell me they're using PPC, my first question is "How much money did it make your company last year?"

Sadly, many companies can't answer this critical question, all because they're not using the right tools.

Case in point: At River Pools, despite the fact we're able to generate a couple million organic website visitors a year to our website, we still engage in pay per click advertising, and here are the results:

In 2015 we spent $12,000 on pay per click, which equated to 11,657 website visitors, 437 leads, 33 sales appointments, and seven customers. These seven customers generated $357,000 in total revenue, with a net profit of just under $100,000.

In other words, for us, PPC is worth it. But had we not been using a tool like HubSpot, this type of data would not be available to us, leading to guesswork and a possible misallocation of marketing funds.

Upon working with our various clients at the Sales Lion, we've seen time and time again that some companies who thought PPC was worth it were losing money, while others who thought PPC didn't make financial sense were missing out on major revenue opportunities.

But PPC is just one example of many. The same story could be told for social media. In the world of digital sales and marketing, companies are continually debating the efficacy of social media, yet few are actually able to say, "Because of Facebook, we generated a net profit of $X,XXX,XXX for our company last year."

No company, regardless of how big or small, can "do everything well" with content, social media, PPC, and so on. It is for this reason organizations need to study and measure what truly drives revenue, and use that data to help them focus more energy and efforts on what's generating the most revenue for the organization while spending less energy and efforts on that which has the smallest returns.

2. The Ability to Track Lead Behavior and Use This Advanced Intelligence throughout the Sales Process

Along with measuring ROI, the other major benefit of using a tool like HubSpot has to do with advanced lead intelligence. And when I say "advanced lead intelligence," I'm specifically referring to having the ability to know what pages of the website a lead has seen, how many times they've visited the site, and how long they spent on each page.

For many sales professionals, the first time they call or contact a lead is a "blind" conversation. In other words, they don't yet know much about the lead, his needs, his hot buttons, and so on. But with advanced lead intelligence, a sales pro can now see every page of the website that individual has read, every video she's watched, and know every time she's come to the site. Digging deeper, each one of these pages is a reflection of what the lead is or is not interested in.

For example, in my case with River Pools, if I saw a lead had visited the "How to Finance a Swimming Pool" page once, I knew they were likely going to need to get financing for their pool. If they looked at the page twice, is was an absolute guarantee they were going to need financing.

By knowing this, I could then work to ensure they had financing taken care of *before* I drove up to their home for the sales appointment, a simple act that would dramatically increase closing rates.

The key to remember here is that every lead has his or her own story—a story that writes itself as the lead engages your content, thus showing you what truly matters and what does not.

For any seasoned sales professional, this type of knowledge and intelligence is very, very appealing.

3. The Ability to Track SEO

Unfortunately, some people in the digital marketing space would say SEO (search engine optimization) is dead. But until the day arrives where we're not using Google (or another search engine), the statement is grossly false and frankly irresponsible. For every client we've had at the Sales Lion, SEO has had a major impact on their ability to generate more traffic, leads, and sales. Sure, in some industries or cases social media or other apps may have a bigger impact on buyers than SEO, but as a whole, consumer research through search engines is going to be a major factor in the success of businesses big and small for years to come.

It is for this reason that you, as a business, must be aware of where you stand in the eyes of Google. You should know the major phrases buyers are searching in your space (Big 5 especially) and you should strive to be the company that is shown when someone searches these phrases.

As we've discussed, They Ask, You Answer is the key to giving yourself a shot at ranking for these phrases, but at the same time, you need a tool to help you quickly see where you rank with each of these and whether you're gaining or losing keyword rankings as you go.

Having a tool like HubSpot, as well as other keyword tools, can help you do just that.

To give you a tangible example of what I'm talking about, with River Pools we currently track more than eight hundred different phrases (like "fiberglass pools" or "inground pool cost") in HubSpot, and currently are ranking in the first three results of Google on more than six hundred of these phrases, which is why you can pretty much go to Google right now, ask a question about a fiberglass swimming pool, and find our website waiting to teach you the answer.

4. The Ability to Test Your Website

The last major benefit of using of using an advanced analytics tool like HubSpot is your ability to test what is and what is not working on your website to convert more leads.

For example, most websites have various "call-to-action" statements or buttons (like "click here" or "download now") sprinkled throughout the site. Notwithstanding, most companies never test these calls-to-action to see how such things as the color of the button, or the wording used, affects conversion rates (how often someone fills out a form).

With our clients at the Sales Lion, we've seen time and time again situations when we thought a page's copy, design, or call-to-action were just right, only to make some minor changes and see a major lift in lead conversions in the process.

Too often, we look at a website and because we think "it looks right" that it's performing at its highest level.

The reality is the best companies understand that just because something *looks* right doesn't mean it *is* right, nor does it mean changes aren't needed.

By having a culture of testing within the digital side of your business, you'll see again and again that the simplest changes in words, messaging, colors, and design matter—and therefore deserve your attention as a business.

This chapter could easily have been much longer, especially with the rate of change in tools and technology today. It's also important to note that HubSpot is only one of many types of software that give you the ability to do the things we discussed. That being said, the core theme is that *we should all be measuring*, so that at any point in your efforts to become the thought leader of your space and embrace They Ask, You Answer you're able to say:

"We put in a lot of work, but we know how much money it made. And it was well worth it."

PART IV

Your Questions Answered

The title of this book, as you well know by this point, is *They Ask, You Answer.* I've discussed these principles with hundreds of organizations around the world, and I'm pretty certain you still have a few questions about them. And nine and a half times out of ten, I've heard them and answered them many times before. In this final part of the book, I address and answer the most frequently asked questions I've received from companies time and time again.

Simply put, it is my goal as the author to help you through what you've learned herein—assuming you're interested—to immediately commence your own content marketing efforts following the guidelines suggested in this book.

In order to do this, you likely need a few additional pointers on some of the detailed questions that most organizations ask as they're getting started. Specifically, we address the following:

1. How do companies find more time to make content marketing work for them?
2. How long will it take content marketing (following the principles of They Ask, You Answer) to work? (that is, generate more traffic, leads, and sales while positively affecting the company brand and bottom line).
3. Is all of this just a fad that's not going to be relevant in twenty years?

4. How do I keep my team engaged and interested in this process? How do I transform it from a program to a culture?
5. What are some of the general guidelines for great content (text, video, and the like)?
6. How does social media play into all of this?

38

How Do I Find More Time to Make This Work within My Organization?

Far and away, one of the most common reasons companies say they haven't been able to achieve success with content marketing comes down to this variable: *Time*.

Individuals and companies are struggling—mightily—to find the time to produce content.

And I get that.

It's not necessarily easy.

It won't happen overnight.

But, when done right, it's always worth it.

This being said, there are absolutely ways you can produce more content, at a faster rate, and more effectively. Some have been touched on already in this book. Others have not. Either way, they all work, as we've done them with our clients many times.

Every Single E-mail You Ever Send Out That Answers a Question Very Well May Be a Blog Post

I'm amazed at just how much content (through e-mail) the average business produces in a day. So many of these e-mails are to prospects and customers, answering their questions, giving them the information they seek. Sadly, most of this content is never used again.

One might call it a "content marketing tragedy."

Here at The Sales Lion, we've seen client content production explode simply by adding one step to their educational (They Ask, You Answer) e-mails—bcc:ing someone in the marketing department so as to ensure that the content (assuming it's a fit) gets used in the future. By simply adding this click of a mouse, content ideas are continually being generated, the marketing team keeps its fingers on the pulse of all the questions and issues the sales team are dealing with, and silos are torn down.

It's powerful. Do it.

Start Talking to Yourself Out Loud—a Lot

We live in the digital age. At this point, we can drive down the road, talk into our phone as if it were a customer, and have it record everything we say. We can then send that recording to a transcription company, who in turn quickly sends us a text-based copy, and voilà—a blog article has been written.

Considering most business owners are better talkers than writers, this is a powerful way of producing a lot of solid content, fast. Of course, this isn't the only way to do it; someone in the content department can easily do a sit-down interview with a thought leader, ask them questions, and walk away with plenty of valuable content.

Participate in Blogathons or Videoathons with Employees

If you have employees and want to create a lot of content in a short period of time, a blogathon just might be the perfect solution. By getting everyone in the office away from writing e-mails and assigning articles and videos to work on—all together and at one time—a company can truly do amazing things. At The Sales Lion, we had one company in the financial space produce more than fifty pieces of content in one day—all because they set aside the time among their team to get it done, without distraction.

Get a Content Manager . . . Yesterday

We already mentioned this one in chapter 36, but it's simply too important not to re-emphasize. Someone must own the content marketing efforts within the company, and that same person is key in getting everyone else involved.

Insourcing Is Huge

Remember, if they are a subject matter expert of any type, and spend any time at all communicating with clients and customers, they could be producing content for your organization right now—all they need is the platform and guidance to do so.

Learn How Each Employee Best Communicates, and Then Run with It

Great content marketing companies understand that not everyone communicates the same way. Some prefer to write it out. Some prefer to talk it out. Some would rather act it out on video.

Smart content marketing companies identify how their employees communicate and encourage each individual to contribute to the process in the way they convey information the best. Some people are great at researching, interviewing, and writing; others are great at performing in front of a camera; and others may not be great at either, but because of their knowledge make great interviewees. In short, when you leverage the strengths of every team member, you can dramatically reduce the time you spend in the production process as well as get the most bang for your buck along the way.

Turn On the Camera and Hit "Record"

Some of our greatest successes I had with my swimming pool company occurred when my business partner Jason and I would walk onto a job site, look around, and just start explaining everything we saw. In a few hours time, we had produced multiple videos, many of which today have hundreds of thousands of views on YouTube.

Keep in mind, most of these videos weren't planned out. We simply looked at the job, asked ourselves what the consumer might want to know or ask, and then began talking.

This principle can be applied to any business, and, boy, does it save some serious time in the process.

Stop Doing the Thing That Does Not Bring the Greatest Returns

Every company has inefficiencies. This is certainly the case with marketing departments as well. Often we are doing marketing and advertising campaigns because we think "we're supposed to," not because there is a clear strategic purpose—one that has been proven to get powerful results.

If most companies had any idea just how much financial impact a smart content marketing campaign would have on their organizations, they would drop in a heartbeat much of what they are currently doing from a business development and marketing perspective.

Is It about Time, or Is There Something Else Really Going On Here?

As humans, when we do not value something enough, we have a simple fallback response:

"I don't have the time."

Granted, sometimes this statement is true.

But the majority of cases I've seen are cut and dried: the company's leadership team didn't "get it." They didn't truly understand content marketing and They Ask, You Answer. They didn't see its potential impact and were not emotionally invested.

When I was about to lose my company in 2009 and working well over sixty hours a week, I didn't have time to write articles and produce videos to put on our company website.

So I stopped watching TV.

I went from eight to six hours of sleep a night.

I looked for every extra second to create more content.

And I did all of this because I didn't have a choice. I was looking over the cliff, simply trying to do anything I could do to hang on.

I'm not implying that you (the reader) fall into this category, but please make sure to ask yourself if it truly is about "time" or if something quite different is the issue at hand.

39 | Just How Important Is Video to Inbound and Content Marketing? How Does It Relate to They Ask, You Answer?

Folks, video is *big*.

And when it comes to They Ask, You Answer, video (and visually-based content) in many ways is dramatically more important than textual-based content.

And if you don't believe me, just look at these fifteen incredible stats, as reported by Insivia in 2016:

1. According to a report published by Forrester, including video in an e-mail leads to a whopping 200–300 percent increase in click-through rates.

2. Unbounce reports that include video on a landing page can increase conversion by 80 percent.

3. YouTube reports mobile video consumption rises 100 percent every year.

4. According to *Rhythm and Insights*, combining video with full-page ads boost engagement by 22 percent.

5. Seventy percent of executives watch work-related videos on business websites at least once a week.

6. Sixty-five percent of executives visit the marketer's website, and 39 percent call a vendor after viewing a video, according to *Forbes*.

7. 147 million Americans watch video on the Internet, according to Nielsen.

8. After watching a video, 64 percent of users are more likely to buy a product online, according to ComScore.

9. 96 percent of B2B organizations use video in some capacity in their marketing campaigns, of which 73 percent report positive results to their ROI, according to a survey conducted by ReelSEO.

10. One-third of all online activity is spent watching video.

11. According to *Forbes*, 59 percent of executives would prefer to watch video than read text.

12. Fifty percent of executives look for more information after seeing a product or service in a video, according to *Forbes*.

13. According to Implix, an introductory e-mail that includes a video receives an increase in click-through rates of 96 percent.

14. *Mist Media* reports that the average Internet user spends 88 percent more time on a site with video.

15. Including a video on your homepage can increase conversion rates by 20 percent or more, according to ReelSEO.

Mind-blowing, wouldn't you agree?

Yet, certainly consistent with every stat, trend, and story we've discussed in this book up to this point.

Furthermore, if we were to report on these exact same topics and behaviors a year from now, the numbers would dwarf what's written here.

It is for this reason that every company—big or small—must not only embrace what is happening with video, but integrate it into every element of their business.

Everyone Is a Media Company

The most successful companies and brands of the digital age understand this reality: Everyone is a media company, whether they like it or not.

In other words, consumers and buyers don't care if you or I "like" a video or not.

They don't care if we watch videos.

They don't care if we have employees who are, or are not, willing to be on camera.

And they certainly don't care if we know how to make a video in the first place.

But here's what they do care about: They care about having their questions and concerns answered. They care about seeing what they're going to spend their money on. They care about how it works, what it feels like, and what it looks like.

Case in point: As I write this book I'm in the process of buying my second boat, a "walkaround" (a fishing boat with a lower cabin for storage, sleeping, and so on) that's between 31 feet and 35 feet long.

Up to this point, I've spent hours analyzing different brands and their product lines. At last count, I had visited at least twenty different boat manufacturer websites. But through all of this, I've been utterly disappointed.

Why?

Because these brands, some of which are extremely large, multimillion-dollar companies, don't get me. They aren't in tune with what I—a relatively experienced fisherman—want to see to be able to feel like I "know" the product.

Instead, what they want to show me is a bunch of pomp-like videos (assuming they even have videos on their website) of their boats going through the water at 50 miles per hour and people sitting on the deck and smiling at each other.

Sure, this is all fine and dandy, but in my case, I don't need to see what a boat looks like going through the water. I don't need to see photos of a family enjoying themselves. Heck, I've already been living that with my own family for quite a while, so it's not going to get my juices flowing.

What will get my juices flowing?

Showing me every nook and corner (via video) of the cabin. I want to see the materials, close-ups of the bedding, the details in the bathroom, and the workmanship on the ceiling.

I want to see the main cockpit, and how each and every knob, button, and piece of hardware works to improve the boating experience.

And out of all the brands that I've looked at, only one—Boston Whaler—has done a truly great job helping me experience what it's like to truly "see" the boat—which is also why I know it (the Conquest 345 model) is the next boat I'm going to buy.

If They Can't See It, It Doesn't Exist

Folks, this is the essence of They Ask, You Answer, and it's exactly why, going forward, it's practically impossible to spend enough time, resources, effort, and energy on video.

At this point, you have to look at it this way:

In the eyes of the consumer, if they can't see it, it doesn't exist.

To help you understand what I mean by this, let's analyze my two companies.

River Pools and Spas is a media company that happens to build and install fiberglass swimming pools.

The Sales Lion is a media company that happens to consult with businesses and brands on their digital sales and marketing efforts.

Do you see how this works?

And because we see ourselves as media companies, we've gone so far as to hire a full-time videographer for each.

Is this cheap? No, but the cost of inaction, and of not embracing what the consumer wants, is dramatically more expensive than the cost of hiring the right people and creating a culture of visual teaching and storytelling, which is exactly what we've done at both companies.

Furthermore, unlike many companies that think all video has to be perfect or "Hollywood" to publish, we understand there are times for super, high-quality video, and there are also times for simple, create-it-on-the-fly content. Our only goal, throughout the entire process of becoming a media company and producing visual content, is to get better and better and better, which is exactly what we're doing.

But we also understand we're still at the beginning of utilizing the power of video to gain consumer trust and business. We see a future in which virtual reality makes our videos of today seem like a technological horse and buggy of tomorrow.

Are the prospects of learning a whole new technology daunting? Sure, but we know there will come a day when, again, the consumer won't care. They will expect virtual reality, and if they don't get it, they will leave.

In our case, we will be ready for them.

It is my hope you will be too.

We Must Show It

Our obsession, regardless of B2B, B2C, and so on, needs to be the same:

- We need to show our story, not just tell it.
- We need to show our employees and their subject matter expertise, not just write about it.
- We need to show our company culture, not just explain it.
- We need to show the what, how, when, where, and why.
- And if we do this, we'll be seen as the expert.
- We'll be the trusted voice.

This is the essence of video and They Ask, You Answer.

40

How Long Will It Take They Ask, You Answer to Work?

"So, if we embrace content marketing as a company, and truly follow They Ask, You Answer as you're telling us, what does success look like? And how long would you expect this to take?"

This, quite possibly, is the number 1 question companies have when they're looking to embrace this business philosophy.

But the question makes sense. Creating a culture of listening, teaching, and then acting upon it isn't easy. It takes time, tools, resources, and major dedication.

It's also quite worth it when done right.

Doing Content Marketing the "Right" Way

As you might imagine, the following is a guideline that can vary dramatically from company to company, and industry to industry. Also, what you're reading here is purely contingent on doing content marketing the "right" way—as explained in this book. Specifically, the following assumes that your company is:

1. Producing at an absolute minimum two to three new pieces of content each week (videos, articles, and so on).
2. Following the philosophies of They Ask, You Answer (a willingness to truly address the most common buying questions a prospect or customer is going to ask, that is, about costs, problems, comparisons, reviews, and so on).
3. The company is fully participating. From management to sales to marketing, everyone is involved, and a mission statement (stating the vision of They Ask, You Answer for your company) has been established.

Five Stages of Content Marketing Success

Assuming you're willing to do these three things, here is a realistic five-stage, three-year time frame and measuring stick of success:

1. Hit "Publish" and get the sales team engaged.
2. Searchers and search engines realize you exist.
3. Finally . . . you get leads.
4. Generate sales and revenue.
5. The snowball is rolling down the mountain.

Stage 1. Months 1–3: Hit "Publish" and Get the Sales Team Engaged

Rarely do amazing things happen in content marketing without an incredibly consistent production and editorial calendar. For many companies, this is, for whatever reason, a major hurdle they've never been able to overcome. But the successful organizations have identified someone on staff who owns the content production process (content manager), their employees from other departments (sales, management, and others) are involved sales and the content "machine" is starting to run nicely. Although this process won't happen overnight, it is realistic to expect it to take place within the first thirty to ninety days after launch.

Also, keep in mind there are immediate victories that can, and should, occur within the first ninety days. For example, if you're producing Big 5 content, then you're clearly addressing the top questions your sales team is receiving. This content should be integrated into the sales process as soon as it's produced.

Remember, every piece of content produced should be viewed as another tool in the sales team's toolbox.

Stage 2. Months 2–5: Searchers and Search Engines Realize You Exist

The majority of business websites, at least before they embrace content marketing, are relatively static (same old information, few changes). Because of this, they get little respect from searchers (consumers) and search engines alike. Furthermore, if a website's age is new (or very young), it gets even less respect from search engines from a keyword ranking standpoint.

But once a company shows a true dedication to content production, and is sticking with its editorial calendar, respect from both parties occurs. Not only are viewers impressed, but search engines are as well.

What does this mean? A few things: Your website's SEO will improve (more keyword phrases will start to rank well), Google will index your site more often, and the speed at which your content starts to produce results will increase. Sure, this usually doesn't happen until the 60–150 day mark, but when it does occur it's the first sign that traffic, leads, and sales are on the cusp of a continual increase for months to come.

Note: A major factor that dictates your ability to have search engines recognize your content involves how saturated your niche or industry already is. In industries where everyone is producing content (like digital marketing companies), it's difficult to rank well in search engines. But among those industries that produce much less content, the lack of competition allows for quicker results.

Regardless of the amount of content saturation, though, your company should still strive to become the most trusted and transparent thought leaders of your space. Otherwise, great results are impossible to achieve.

Stage 3. Months 3–6: Finally . . . You Get Leads

Now that traffic is really starting to pick up, it's time for leads. And the whole purpose of content marketing—aside from engaging prospects and customers and building trust—is to increase leads and ultimately generate sales.

Beyond the blog articles and videos, an effective content marketing campaign will include calls-to-action on the site, premium pieces of content (like e-books, white papers, and so on), and other components.

Also, now that leads are starting to come in, keep in mind it's critical to measure where they are coming from. Specifically, you want to always look at your leads and the piece of content that brought them to the site. If that lead at some point becomes a customer, and you know their originating piece of content, you can now track value back to that one single article, video, tweet, and so on. As you might imagine, your ability to do this is critical for the long-term success and buy-in of your content marketing efforts. It also shows you where you need to spend more or less of your time, resources, and attention.

Stage 4. Months 4–18: Generate Sales and Revenue

Finally, the day has come: you were able to track an actual sale back to your content marketing efforts. The importance of this transaction, and every one after this, is critical to the long-term success of the content and making it a culture.

Depending on your company's sales cycles, along with a variety of other factors, the speed at which sales result from your content marketing efforts can vary tremendously. That being said, it should certainly happen before the first-year mark. Furthermore, sales teams should be getting better and better by this point at using the content that has been produced and injecting it throughout the prospect's entire sales experience.

Stage 5. Months 18–36: The Snowball Is Rolling Down the Mountain

For the first year or so, establishing an ultra-successful content marketing program can almost feel like you're rolling a snowball up a mountain. Frankly, it's no easy task.

But there does come a point, especially if you do it consistently and the right way, focusing on They Ask, You Answer (and allowing that to guide future strategy), that the snowball will not only reach the top of the mountain, but it will start rolling down the other side, picking up momentum and growing bigger than your wildest expectations.

Many of the case studies you've read in this book were certainly examples of this phenomena.

But it took time. It took people willing to own the program and management teams who made it clear to the team just how serious the content marketing efforts were.

Regardless of your industry or the size of your company, I truly believe these types of results are available for you. As you have already surmised, these numbers are all estimates. There are too many factors to list and too many variables in every company and industry to come up with hard numbers.

That being said, these parameters will, I hope, guide you along your content marketing journey and help you have a clearer vision of what to expect ahead.

41

Is Content Marketing and They Ask, You Answer Just a Fad?

"Will content marketing even be around in ten years once everyone has attempted to do it?"

This question, and others just like it, have been tossed my way in almost every presentation I've given on the subject over the past five years.

And unfortunately, for many of the folks asking the question, this lack of understanding as to what content marketing really is has led to inaction and a greater divide between themselves and their competitors—those who *are* willing to accept today's consumer and shift the way they market and sell accordingly.

What Exactly Is Content Marketing?

Fundamentally, if we boil it down to its most basic characteristics, how would we define *content marketing* (assuming we weren't using marketing speak)?

- Earning trust through teaching?
- Using great information to help others solve their problems?
- Listening to consumer questions and providing honest answers to those questions?

However you define it, these basic tenets of content marketing and They Ask, You Answer have been around *forever*. Since the beginning of time, we've known that great communication, listening, teaching, and transparency all lead to trust.

The same could be said for the future.

But today, because of the Internet and the information age, we've given it a name: content marketing. It's not a name I made up, and it's maybe not even the name we'll be using in twenty or thirty years. But it certainly fits the bill for right now to describe this act of using helpful and utilitarian information to earn trust with the digital consumer.

In the future, what will change about the way consumers develop trust with brands and ultimately make buying decisions?

- Will teaching still be relevant?
- Will helping others solve their problems still hold value and build trust?
- Will it be important to obsessively hear and address questions from your prospects and customers?

Yes, of course they will.

Consumers will be vetting businesses like yours and mine more deeply than they ever have before.

And when they stumble across a website (or whatever we call it in the future) that is truly a resource and a wealth of knowledge, they will stay.

So is what we're talking about herein a fad?

Nope, it's a principle that has been around since the beginning and is not going anywhere anytime soon.

42

How Can I Keep My Team Engaged in the Content Production Process?

In order to overcome this issue and help your team produce the type and amount of content they are capable of, it's critical to get creative. Simply saying, "Everyone, start blogging," will never be enough, at least not in developing a culture in which creating content is not simply something team members check off each month. There must be more.

Krista Kotrla of Block Imaging, whom we discussed in chapter 34, has created a masterful culture of getting consistent participation from dozens and dozens of employees in the effort to produce consistent, powerful company content. The following is a list inspired by some of the things she has done to keep the magic of They Ask, You Answer going at Block Imaging, as well as some of the other creative ways clients have made this such a successful culture.

Ten Ways to Keep Your Employees Motivated to Participate in Content Marketing

1. Focus Your Initial Content on the Bottom-of-the-Funnel Buyer Questions and Get It in the Hands of the Sales Team

Remember, quick wins are essential to great content marketing, and one of the mistakes many teams make is starting off with questions that won't generate immediate results, at least not from a SEO or sales standpoint. This is why addressing the subjects of the Big 5: cost, problems, comparisons, reviews, and best-of are generally the most critical to tackle early on in the content marketing process. Once completed, you'll take these same pieces of content, stack them together in an organized way, and create e-books, guides, video series, and so on so as to enhance the sales team's capabilities to educate the prospect, earn trust, and close more deals.

2. Shine a Light On the Superhero Participants by Giving Them Awards and Team Recognition

Publicly tell the stories of why team members are being recognized so that others will learn from their example and, one hopes, want to copy them. Remember, if you can make the employees (especially those in the sales department) look like rock stars, others will naturally want to be a part of the "movement" as well.

3. Encourage the Team to Share Cross-Department Successes in Meetings

Create a segment for *others* to tell their success stories. It is really powerful when these experiences start popping up in other departments. An example of this would be a salesperson thanking an engineer for the blog article that was the catalyst for a lead contacting the company and ultimately turning into a customer.

4. Share Results and Celebrate Milestones

You can customize awards and recognition for your situation, but here are a few examples of milestones worth celebrating:

- Articles or videos that reach a thousand views
- Number of leads generated
- Views from organic traffic
- When you finally rank on page 1 of search results for target keyword phrases
- Share recent deals and tie them back to the content that played into the customer experience

Note: A great way to do this in a consistent, organized manner is to create a quarterly newsletter that everyone on the team can read and see all of the highlights from that time period.

5. Create Some Team Goals to Strive Toward Together

Here are examples of activities you could consider:

- *Individual*: Five blog articles = slippers (something visible that they get to wear around the office like a status symbol)
- *Collective*: Two hundred blogs = whirly ball (everyone gets to go play)
- *Department versus department competition* (service team versus product team)
- *Individual versus individual face-off*

6. Make They Ask, You Answer Training Part of the Hiring and Onboarding Process for New Team Members in Every Department

This goes without saying, but it's critical. Also, if you have an initial all-hands-on-deck workshop to kick off your inbound and content marketing efforts, make sure you video record it for future employees.

7. *Make It Easy for the Team to Share Content*

Want your employees to share content? Make it easy for them. Teach them how to do it. For example, you could introduce them to:

- *Lazy links*: A hyperlink to a website typed in by an instant messenger chat member while chatting because he or she is too lazy to open up a browser, type in the URL, and click "enter."
- *E-mail signatures*: One of the simplest ways to point someone's attention to content, especially with all new signature tools available on the market today.
- *Social media*: Many more employees would share company content if they understood how to share it, when to share it, and why to share it. A little training can go a long way in this process.

8. *Ask for Help in Very Specific Ways*

Remember, everyone wants to feel important, which is why "special tasks" or "missions" can be a great content marketing initiative. Here are a few examples:

"Hey, here's a strategic phrase that we don't rank for yet and is an area you know a lot about. Could you address this topic so that people will find us when searching for this answer?"

"Hey, Manager, we're not seeing any content from your department lately. Could you bring this up in your next team meeting to drum up some activity and participation? Your department is full of knowledge, and we need to get that knowledge out to the rest of the world."

"Hey, we're going to take all of your greatest blog articles and start filming video versions as well. We want people to not just hear you, but see you as well. Here is a meeting invite for your first filming session."

9. *Humanize It*

Always remind everyone of the real human beings that this content affects. How does it change lives? What is the deeper "why" to what they're being asked to do?

10. Stay Curious

Great content marketing leaders are always looking for an edge. Part of this is never being satisfied with average and doing whatever it takes to become a world-class organization of teachers and listeners. A big part of this is knowing how to ask the right questions of your team. Here are a few examples:

> "Hey, you're really awesome at generating content on a regular basis. What is your secret to making it look easy? How have you worked it in to your everyday life?"
>
> "Hey, thought you'd be interested to learn that 80 percent of your team members are contributing content. I'm curious to hear how I can make it easier for you to participate so that people can learn from you too."
>
> "How can I make this easier for the team to participate? How can I make it more fun?"
>
> "How can I prove this is working?

The bottom line to great content and They Ask, You Answer is this, folks: It's about results. This is exactly why you must get results, then tell the results, then celebrate the results, and, of course, improve results. *And*, while doing this, tell the stories that help everyone remember that this is about *real people*.

Sometimes you have to lead by example. Sometimes you have to get in the trenches and work side by side. You have to empower others to equip and encourage one another. You have to set up a lot of feedback loops. You have to love the challenge of it. You have to build it into your culture.

No, it's not easy, but it is certainly worth it.

43

"I've Been Told If We're Not Adding Anything New to the Conversation, Then We Shouldn't Be Talking about It"

One of the biggest tragedies I've seen spoken out of the mouths of "experts" in the digital marketing space is the concept that if someone (individual, company, or other entity) has already said (written about, talked about, produced a video about) something, then it's a waste of time for someone else to add their two cents, especially if they're not adding anything "new" to the conversation.

For lack of a better way of putting this: the people who make these statements are ignorant of the history of the world and completely missing the mark.

You see, at this point (in the 21st century), most everything we say is a repeat of what someone else has already said.

In this book, I've espoused honesty, transparency, and great teaching so as to gain trust in business.

Is this a new concept?

No, it's older than dirt.

But I'm explaining it my way, with my stories, in my language.

And because I'm willing to take the time to explain it in the pages herein, two parties benefit.

First of all, for many readers, this may be the book that finally touches them in such a way that they take action by becoming obsessive listeners, problem solvers, and teachers in their space—something that will generate more trust and ultimately new business.

This increase in business will lead to increased revenues, enable them to hire more employees, and ideally live a life of financial peace.

You might read those words and think I'm exaggerating, but I'm not. I've seen the results of this again and again. I've been talking about the importance of They Ask, You Answer for more than five years. I've been blogging about it, producing videos about it, and speaking on stages around the world about it.

I've seen what can happen when individuals and businesses embrace this philosophy, many of whom have contacted me after the fact and told me touching stories of the impact—personally and professionally.

This brings me to the other party that benefits: me.

By writing this book, I'm being forced to take everything I've learned and distill it into words. I've been challenged to research deeper, think harder, and articulate my thoughts and experiences more clearly.

And because of this, I will finish this book a better communicator on this subject than I was when I started.

You see, that is the thing—by producing content, regardless of how many times "it has been said"—we become better people, better employees, better sales professionals, and better communicators.

That's how it works.

And that's how it has worked for thousands of years.

Before I finish my thoughts on this subject, just look at the most popular book of all time: the Bible.

Anyone who has read the Books of Mathew, Mark, Luke, and John of the New Testament know these Gospels are very similar. In fact, there is quite a bit of redundancy across the four books.

But what would have happened if Luke had said, "Well, Mathew already talked about this, so I think it would be a waste of time for me to talk about it as well"?

History would have changed entirely.

Regardless of your thoughts on the Gospels, I hope you see my point here.

This is why I truly believe every individual and company needs to write what I call "The Gospel According to *You*."

- Your prospects and customers want to know your thoughts and feelings.
- They want to know what you believe and why you believe it.
- But *you* also need to experience this as well.
- You need to distill your thoughts.
- You need to state your company's doctrine.

By so doing, you'll positively affect every party involved. You'll become better teachers and communicators. You'll be more in touch with what your customers are thinking.

And you'll gain their trust.

44

A Revolutionary Marketing Strategy

As I look back on these past seven years, it almost seems like a dream.

One day, I'm a pool guy on the brink of losing my business. The bank is calling. My credit cards are maxed out. My employees are sitting home. And as a father and husband, I'm failing.

And then, what seems like the next day I'm traveling the world and helping businesses become their best selves while speaking to audiences of hundreds and thousands of people. It's amazing. Really amazing. And more important, as a father and husband, I'm present. Believe it or not, I'm home way more now than I ever was as a struggling pool guy.

Simply put, we are happy. We are blessed.

In many ways, how the River Pools and Spas story became so very well known in the digital space occurred when I experienced a very fortunate event in 2013.

That year, I was speaking at a conference in Dallas, Texas. After my talk, a reporter came up to me and said he would like to do a story on how we were able to save River Pools through such a simple strategy as listening, teaching, and transparency.

Frankly, I didn't think much of this reporter's request until we spoke on the phone for ninety minutes a few days later.

Then, a few days after that, he sent a photographer to my swimming pool company.

And what happened next is where my life very much changed.

Four days after the photographer showed up at River Pools and Spas, the following article appeared on the cover of the small business section of the *New York Times*:

If you look at the article, you'll notice a peculiar irony.

Notice how the title is "A *Revolutionary* Marketing Strategy: Answer Customers' Questions."

Folks, is there really anything "revolutionary" about answering your customer's questions?

In principle, no.

But in practice? Yes, absolutely.

This became the number 1 shared and e-mailed story for the small business section of the *Times* during the next three days. They even re-ran the article as a blog post on Saturday that same week.

Without question, the story resonated.

In fact, I was shocked to find it resonated so much that over the coming months I got more than a thousand e-mails from business owners and marketers all over the world.

What's funny, though, is that almost all of these e-mails said one of two things.

The first comment everyone wanted to make was,

"Marcus, that thing you did with your pool company is so simple. I just can't believe how simple it is!"

Yes, it was simple.

But simple is good. This way, anyone, including you, can apply what we did at River Pools and Spas to your business. You just have to truly care enough about the consumer to obsessively listen, teach, solve problems, and be honest in the process.

The second main comment I got from people who had read the article sounded like this:

"Marcus, I feel like you've now given me permission to do that which I've always felt we should be doing."

This one, to me, is the crux of the whole thing.

Throughout this book, if you've made it to this point, there assuredly have been many times where you've thought to yourself, *I've been feeling like we should be doing this for a long time.*

So now, as we come to a close, I ask you to follow the promptings you've already been getting. After all, we get them for a reason.

- Be the best teacher in the world.
- Obsess over their questions.
- Answer with fierce honesty.
- And win their trust.

Index